The Seafarers THE
NORTHWEST
PASSAGE

TIME
LIFE ®
BOOKS

*This volume is one of a series
that celebrates the history of
maritime adventure, from the Greek
trireme to the modern ocean liner.*

The Cover: Winding through loose pack ice
in early September, 1850, the 400-ton
Investigator, captained by British explorer
Robert McClure, nears Banks Island, at
the eastern edge of the Beaufort Sea. The
ship was later trapped in ice, but her
crew managed to make the first transit of the
Northwest Passage—partly on foot.

The Title Page: Standard equipment for
nautical explorers venturing into the Arctic
from the late 18th Century on was an
ice grapnel, used to warp a ship through
passages between floes. Attached to a
hawser, the grapnel was taken out in front of
the vessel and hooked to the ice; the
hawser was then reeled in by means of the
capstan, pulling the ship forward.

The Seafarers

THE NORTHWEST PASSAGE

by Brendan Lehane

AND THE EDITORS OF TIME-LIFE BOOKS

TIME-LIFE BOOKS, ALEXANDRIA, VIRGINIA

The Seafarers

Editorial Staff for *The Northwest Passage:*
Editor: Anne Horan
Designer: Herbert H. Quarmby
Picture Editor: Marion F. Briggs
Text Editors: Roberta Conlan, Deborah Berger-Turnbull
Staff Writers: Carol Dana, Lee Greene
Researchers: Patti H. Cass, Susan Kelly,
Mindy A. Daniels, Therese A. Daubner, Roxie France,
Adrienne George, Ann Dusel Kuhns,
Anne Muñoz-Furlong, Jo Thomson
Art Assistant: Robert K. Herndon
Editorial Assistant: Cathy A. Sharpe

Special Contributors
Martha Reichard George, Barbara Hicks (research)

Editorial Production
Production Editor: Douglas B. Graham
Operations Manager: Gennaro C. Esposito,
Gordon E. Buck (assistant)
Assistant Production Editor: Feliciano Madrid
Quality Control: Robert L. Young (director), James J. Cox
(assistant), Daniel J. McSweeney, Michael G. Wight
(associates)
Art Coordinator: Anne B. Landry
Copy Staff: Susan B. Galloway (chief), Anne T. Connell,
Victoria Lee, Celia Beattie
Picture Department: Betsy Donahue
Traffic: Kimberly K. Lewis

Correspondents: Elisabeth Kraemer (Bonn); Margot
Hapgood, Dorothy Bacon, Lesley Coleman (London);
Susan Jonas, Lucy T. Voulgaris (New York); Maria
Vincenza Aloisi, Josephine du Brusle (Paris); Ann
Natanson (Rome).
Valuable assistance was also provided by Katrina Van
Duyn (Copenhagen); Janet Zich (Half Moon Bay,
California); Enid Farmer (Lexington, Massachusetts);
Caroline Alcock, Judy Aspinall, Karin B. Pearce, Pippa
Pridham (London); Carolyn T. Chubet, Miriam Hsia,
Christina Lieberman (New York); Bent Onsager (Oslo);
John Scott (Ottawa); Mimi Murphy (Rome); Ed Ogle
(Vancouver); Gord Sinclair (Winnipeg).

The Author:
Brendan Lehane was born in London of
Irish parents in 1936. After he graduated
from Cambridge University, he worked for
two years on magazines and in book publishing, traveled for a year in Africa and
then became a freelance writer. His books
include *The Companion Guide to Ireland*,
The Complete Flea, *The Power of Plants*,
and *Dublin* in The Great Cities series for
Time-Life Books.

The Consultants:
John Horace Parry, Gardiner Professor of
Oceanic History and Affairs at Harvard,
obtained his Ph.D. from Cambridge University. He is the author of many books on
seafaring, among them *The Discovery of
the Sea* and *Trade and Dominion*.

David B. Quinn, Professor of History at
St. Mary's College of Maryland, is the author of a number of books about pioneering
voyages across the Atlantic Ocean, including *North America from Earliest Discovery
to First Settlement*.

David Lyon, educated at King's College,
Cambridge, has participated in underwater
surveys of 18th Century ships and is an au-
thority on historical ships' plans. He is a
member of the board of the Nautical Ar-
chaeological Trust.

For information about any Time-Life book, please write:
Reader Information, Time-Life Books,
541 North Fairbanks Court, Chicago, Illinois 60611.

TIME-LIFE is a trademark of Time Incorporated U.S.A.

Library of Congress Cataloguing in Publication Data
Lehane, Brendan.
The Northwest passage.
  (The Seafarers; 20)
  Bibliography: p.
  Includes index.
  1. Northwest Passage. I. Time-Life Books.
II. Title. III. Series: Seafarers.
G640.L4   910'.0916327   80-27723
ISBN 0-8094-2732-X
ISBN 0-8094-2731-1 (lib. bdg.)
ISBN 0-8094-2730-3 (retail ed.)

Contents

Desolate splendor
of the polar realm

The four-century search for the Northwest Passage, a navigable channel that was believed to connect the North Atlantic and the Pacific Oceans, lured mariners to one of the world's most formidable frontiers. As the survivors of scores of defeated expeditions straggled home from the polar latitudes that were the focus of the hunt, they told of a forbidding but fascinating region of soaring icebergs, glowing skies and a desolation so profound that one explorer described the Arctic as "a world unfinished by the hand of its Creator."

By the mid-19th Century, public curiosity about the far north had reached the point of passion. Arctic adventure became a popular literary theme, and painters created vivid Arctic scenes, generally relying on the explorers' crude drawings plus a substantial degree of imagination. One German artist worked by a form of mental magnification: He observed modest-sized chunks of ice floating down the Elbe River and, on canvas, transformed them into massive icebergs surrounding a tiny ship.

But a handful of dedicated artists ventured northward to see the Arctic at first hand. Among them were two Americans who would earn worldwide reputations for their portrayals of northern icescapes. Frederic Edwin Church contracted a lasting case of Arctic fever when he saw his first icebergs floating off Newfoundland and Labrador in the summer of 1859. Awed by the spectacle, he used enormous canvases to convey the grandeur of the icy edifices and of the dazzling Arctic phenomenon known as the northern lights, or aurora borealis (right).

A painter who roved still farther was William Bradford, son of a New Bedford ship's chandler. Determined "to study Nature under the terrible aspects of the Frigid Zone," he made seven trips to Labrador between 1861 and 1868 before undertaking a three-month, 5,000-mile voyage in 1869 to Melville Bay on the Greenland coast, 600 miles above the Arctic Circle. There, with a matchless feel for the rigors of the Northwest Passage quest, Bradford limned the fields and floes of ice that had thwarted generations of mariners—and that would not permit a sea journey across the top of the world until the early 20th Century.

A lone vessel, iced in for the duration of a sunless Arctic winter, is illuminated by a brilliant display of northern lights in a panorama by Frederic Church. Such streaks of celestial color, peculiar to polar latitudes, result from collisions of charged particles from the sun with gases in the earth's upper atmosphere. The scene is set at Church Peak, an Ellesmere Island mountain named for Church by explorer Isaac Hayes in 1860.

In a vista entitled "Ice Dwellers Watching the Invaders," William Bradford depicts curious seals and polar bears observing the steam whaler Panther off

the Greenland coast in 1869. More than one expedition, running out of food, survived by trading with Eskimos for seal meat and other Arctic provender.

Hemmed in by shifting floes, members of an Arctic expedition use long ice saws in order to cut open a channel for their vessels in this scene

by William Bradford. In the ice-filled waters, ships sometimes took days or even weeks to make their way a few miles.

In a dramatic vision by Frederic Church, the mast of a crushed vessel and a dark boulder ripped from a distant mountain are testimony to the terrible power

of Arctic ice. To do justice to the majesty of icebergs, the artist painted this scene on a canvas more than five feet high and nine feet long.

First encounters with an unexpected barrier

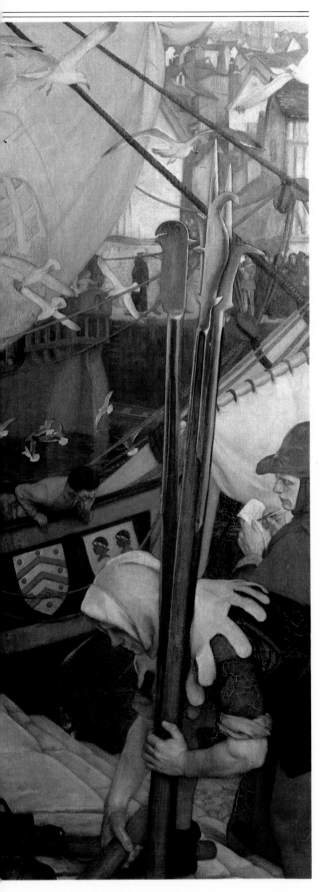

arly on a June morning in the year 1497, a Venetian citizen known to the English as John Cabot first sighted North America from the deck of his 50-ton ship *Mathew*. He and his crew of 18, including some respected merchants of Bristol, were about a month out from England. As the dawn haze lifted, the wooded coastline of what may have been Cape Bauld, Newfoundland, presented them with a tantalizing statement of unknown possibilities. Cabot and his men went ashore and claimed the land for England; in remembrance of his own nationality, Cabot also planted the flag of Saint Mark, the patron saint of Venice.

The explorers soon realized that the land was inhabited: "They saw a site where a fire had been made," an Englishman named John Day later recorded. "They saw manure of animals which they thought to be farm animals, and they saw a stick half a yard long, pierced at both ends, carved and painted with brazil"—a reddish dye. The inhabitants evidently had fled, but Cabot was wary of risking a tiny ship's company against the resources of an unfamiliar country. He walked inland no deeper than "the shooting distance of a crossbow," Day wrote, before returning to the ship.

Despite the lack of evidence, Cabot was convinced he had reached the Orient—perhaps even Japan, the legendary island whose wealth Marco Polo had described as "inexhaustible." He did not doubt that somewhere behind the silent conifers that lined the shore were palaces of gold, a people to whom silk was as workaday as the woolens of England, and priceless mountains of spices. There is no record of how he continued the reconnaissance, but very likely he coasted south for a few hundred miles. Still, all that confronted him was trees, scrub and more signs of rather primitive dwellers. No matter. The proof that this was the territory of the Grand Khan must lie farther on, where the coast snaked its way to tropical latitudes.

For now, the exploration was over; Cabot was running out of provisions and still had 2,500 miles of open sea to retrace. As he doubled back to his original landfall in order to "run his easting down"—the simple navigational technique of locking onto a known latitude for a given port—the *Mathew* plowed through a sea thick with fish. Word of this bountiful ocean would, in due course, draw fishermen from France and Portugal to vie with the English for the rich harvest of cod, sole and halibut to be reaped from the Grand Banks off Newfoundland.

Cabot and the *Mathew* were back in Bristol the first week in August. Their story electrified the port's citizenry, although some people were skeptical: Cabot had brought back not the slightest material surety of his find—no silks or spices, no gold or precious stones. His trophies from the far side of the Atlantic were in fact quite homely: a net and some snares abandoned in a campsite. Indeed, "as a foreigner and a poor

John Cabot accepts the blessings of religious and civil dignitaries as he prepares to embark from Bristol in 1497 on a voyage across the Atlantic to find the silks and spices of Cathay.

man," a Spanish diplomat wrote home, Cabot would not have been believed at all, "had it not been that his companions, who are practically all English and from Bristol, testified that he spoke the truth." But Cabot's own faith in his achievement was firm. He hastened to London to report his findings to his sponsor, King Henry VII.

King Henry's employment of a foreign mariner was not unusual. Several years earlier, the King had missed the chance to sponsor the epochal voyage of Christopher Columbus only because the would-be explorer's petition had been delayed by storms; by the time Henry had learned of his proposal, Columbus had already secured the support of Ferdinand and Isabella of Spain. Then, in March 1496, Cabot had presented the English monarch with a similar petition. To Henry—who deemed Columbus' achievement "a thing more divine than human"—it was opportunity's rare second knock. Some contemporaries described Cabot— Genoa-born like Columbus—as a master navigator, but it seems more likely that he was a landsman with a good grasp of geography and navigation. Well versed in Marco Polo's heady descriptions of Cathay, Cabot was also familiar—as the English on the whole were not—with the teachings of Cardinal Pierre d'Ailly. D'Ailly's *Imago Mundi*, published in 1487, drew upon Classical thinkers such as Seneca and Aristotle for proof that a ship could easily reach Asia by sailing west from Europe. The work had also influenced Columbus, who scribbled scores of notes in the margins of his copy.

John Cabot was a persuasive talker, and Henry VII had been receptive to his petition, but—as the monarch of a country that was still recovering from the 30-year-long War of the Roses—he was not accustomed to making decisions that required dipping too deep into the royal coffers. Fortunately for Cabot, Henry did not have to. Cabot's proposal was backed by a number of Bristol merchants who were willing to foot the bill, provided Bristol was designated the port of entry for the hoped-for spice trade. Since 1480 these merchants had been sending out three or four ships a year to search for Atlantic islands whose existence was the stuff of legend: Atlantis, Antilia and Brazil Rock. But the idea of finding a direct route to China had not occurred to them until John Cabot suggested it. They jumped at the opportunity to make Bristol the nation's major entrepôt for spices.

Relieved of any onerous financial commitment, Henry had granted letters of patent for a voyage of discovery "to our well-beloved John Cabot, citizen of Venice, and to Lewis, Sebastian and Sancio, sons of said John." The letters authorized them to take possession, for the Crown, of any lands "which before this time were unknown to all Christians." And, lo, Cabot had done precisely that.

After hearing his report, the King rewarded Cabot with an annual pension of £20 and the promise of more substantial royal backing for another voyage in the spring. Henry also gave him £10 as pocket money "that he may have a good time until then," as a Venetian diplomat wrote.

So the winter passed, and by the following May, Cabot was ready to sail again. His fleet had burgeoned from one ship to five: Four were outfitted by London and Bristol merchants, and King Henry, true to his word, equipped another. The expedition carried a year's worth of provi-

An aged Sebastian Cabot spreads navigational dividers across the Arctic region of the globe. He claimed the discovery of what he called the "hid secret of nature"—the Northwest Passage— during a voyage there when he was young.

sions, as well as a varied cargo of goods to trade for the spices the explorers were sure to find. Soon after leaving Bristol the fleet ran into bad weather, and one damaged vessel limped into port in Ireland. The rest continued westward across the vast Atlantic, leaving England —and history—behind.

No reliable record of their fate has survived, but a body of circumstantial evidence strongly suggests that some part of Cabot's fleet made landfall again on the far side of the ocean and returned safely. Whoever did come back from the second voyage would have reported the ultimate failure of their mission. For as Cabot continued to sail southwestward along what he believed to be the coast of Asia, he would have found none of the riches he was searching for. Cabot's disappointed Bristol sponsors no doubt wrote off the expedition as a total loss—not even worth the bother of recording.

No more is heard of John Cabot after 1498, but at least one person did not forget the mysterious failure of his two attempts to find the shining cities of Cathay. Sebastian Cabot was about 14 when his father first crossed the Atlantic. He may even have accompanied his father on one of the voyages. Though Sebastian later gained a reputation as a garrulous and boastful fellow whose claims to glory were to be taken with a grain of salt, it seems fairly certain that in 1508, making use of the letters of patent inherited from his father, he outfitted two ships at his own expense and struck out across the ocean. His course took him so far north, wrote the Spanish chronicler Peter Martyr, who came to know Cabot several years later, that "even in the month of July he found great icebergs floating in the sea and almost continuous daylight." Cabot seems to have entered what was later named Hudson Strait. Then his crews apparently mutinied and forced him to turn back toward more temperate climates to the south. It would not be the last time sailors balked at the rigors of northern exploration.

After coasting south perhaps as far as Florida, Cabot returned to England. There he found that Henry VII was dead. The nation's leaders, caught up in coronation festivities for 17-year-old Henry VIII, had no time for reports of another failed attempt to find Cathay.

For a while Cabot may have tried to gain royal support for further explorations, but the young monarch was too interested in consolidating his position in the Old World to waste time on dubious enterprises in the New. Spain was rather annoyed by forays that were getting suspiciously close to its own territories across the Atlantic, and Henry could not risk overtly offending his touchy ally. No English expeditions at all would go to America for nearly 20 years, and no major ones for nearly 70.

Thwarted by Henry's lack of support, Sebastian Cabot moved on to Spain in 1512. There he was given the job of approving pilots, navigation instruments and charts for the convoy routes to the New World. For the next three decades, he quenched his thirst for discovery in the service of the Spanish Crown.

Sebastian Cabot, like his father, had searched in vain for the golden wealth of the Grand Khan. But in voyaging to an icy northern sea he had done something radically different. Sebastian Cabot was probably the first person to propose the existence of a northwest passage through the New World to Cathay. That he was searching for such a passage is indicated by the high latitude of his course. There would have been little point in sailing so far north if Sebastian, like his father, had believed that the shoreline of the New Found Lands—as the English called America—joined that of Cathay somewhere to the south and west. John Cabot's error (and the similar error of Columbus before him) sprang from the general assumption of the time, handed down from Ptolemy, that the earth's circumference measured about 18,000 miles, roughly 7,000 miles less than it actually is. Neither of these courageous navigators could have suspected that between them and their real goal lay not only another continent but an extra ocean as well.

But during the decade that followed John Cabot's second voyage—and perhaps as a result of that voyage—Sebastian Cabot had grasped the truth. In guessing, or simply hoping, that a passage through or around this obstacle might be discovered in the Arctic zone of the continent, he took the first step in one of the most compulsive and quixotic quests in the history of seafaring. Several generations of explorers would follow Sebastian Cabot's example, combing the ice-locked northern waters for the elusive channel.

The route itself long remained locked in the realms of guesswork, optimism and—since those who returned from the Arctic brought mounting testimony to the brutal difficulty of the search—obstinacy. Cut off from the familiar world, often trapped for months in an endless landscape of frozen white, explorers fell prey not only to the unpredictable dangers of the Arctic itself, but to their own explosive emotions. The annals of the quest are full of murder and mutiny. If the northern explorers had been motivated solely by the desire for wealth and honor, they would have cut their losses early and given up. The barren rocks yielded only fool's gold, and there was scant honor in dying of scurvy. Others might come into the icy country in pursuit of whales and beaver, small colonies might eventually take root in the foreign soil—but the men who marked the way in were not, as a rule, either hunters or colonizers by nature. Their quest—one that endured for some four centuries—had to be fueled by something less dependent on material reward: the quintessential human need to render the unknown known, regardless of the outcome.

Whatever their individual reasons, the men who went to the earth's Arctic regions collectively advanced civilization's knowledge of the vast territory at the top of the globe, though progress was often measured in millimeters on a world map. Many returned again and again, for in a search born of ignorance and myth, myth held on with uncanny strength. The next bay or river—or the next—would surely be the longed-for Northwest Passage, the opening to Cathay.

England was not yet a great sea power when the Cabots, father and son, sailed under its flag. Spain and Portugal ruled the waves through much of the 16th Century, thanks in no small part to the connivance of a Spanish-born pope, Alexander VI. After the voyage of Columbus, he had granted Spain possession of all new lands west of an imaginary line in the Atlantic. Portugal received rights to everything east of this line. Already Portugal had a thriving African trade in ivory, pepper, gold and slaves; and in 1497 it gained a near monopoly on trade with the Far East when Vasco da Gama pioneered the passage around Africa to India. As for the Spanish, vigorous exploration in their new territories soon soothed any distemper over not having found the true Indies. In rapid succession, Spain unearthed gold in Hispaniola (the incalculable wealth of the Aztec and Inca would come to light some 30 to 40 years later), pearls and a source of slaves on the coast of Venezuela, and—if not the spices of Asia—such foodstuffs from America as cocoa, potatoes, allspice and chili peppers.

By the 1520s the seemingly endless bounty flowing into the two Iberian treasuries had brewed a covetous envy among nations to the north—enough to undermine whatever weight the papal bull might have carried. The French monarch Francis I, who badly needed money for his war against Charles V of Spain, commissioned Giovanni da Verrazano, a wellborn Florentine in his service, to undertake the country's first expedition to seek the wealth of Cathay by sailing west across the Atlantic. Verrazano left the Old World on January 17, 1524, in the 100-ton ship *Dauphine*. He had a crew of 50—including his younger brother, Girolamo, a cartographer—and provisions for eight months. Heading west from the Portuguese Madeira Islands, he intended to strike the New World north of Columbus' landfall. Patient exploration was slowly filling in the map south of there, but virtually nothing was known of the territory to the north. The continent's western shores might lie as close to Cathay as those of England to France. Or the land mass might not be a continent at all, but merely an archipelago, as Columbus' Indies had turned out to be. The Florentine planned a systematic investigation to determine the truth.

After about six weeks at sea, Verrazano sighted what may have been Cape Romain in what is now South Carolina. Several days later, somewhere between Capes Lookout and Hatteras in North Carolina, he made a miscalculation that earned him a certain amount of ridicule later. For in gazing across "an isthmus a mile in width and 200 long," he wrote, and seeing no sign of land beyond, he believed he was looking at the waters of "the Eastern Ocean"—the Pacific—"the same that flows around the shores of India and China." The waters apparently were too shoal for the navigator to get close enough to discover that his "isthmus"—the Carolina Outer Banks—divided the Atlantic from nothing more spacious than Pamlico and Albemarle Sounds.

Verrazano continued north in high spirits, expecting at any moment to come upon a way through to the Pacific. He missed several likely-looking openings—the Chesapeake and Delaware Bays, for example—but was the first European to anchor in what is now New York Bay: "a very pleasant place," he noted, "situated among certain steep hills." In mid-June, the *Dauphine* reached Nova Scotia. "Having spent all our naval stores and victuals," Verrazano reported, "and having discovered 700 leagues of new country, we topped off with water and wood and decided to return to France."

Within a few years Spanish exploration would discover the truth

In a romanticized 19th Century vista,
French master pilot Jacques Cartier (inset)
ascends the St. Lawrence River with
Indian guides in 1535. Any hopes that the
great waterway was the Northwest
Passage had long since disappeared by the
time he approached the site of present-
day Montreal, where even his longboats
were turned back by the rapids.

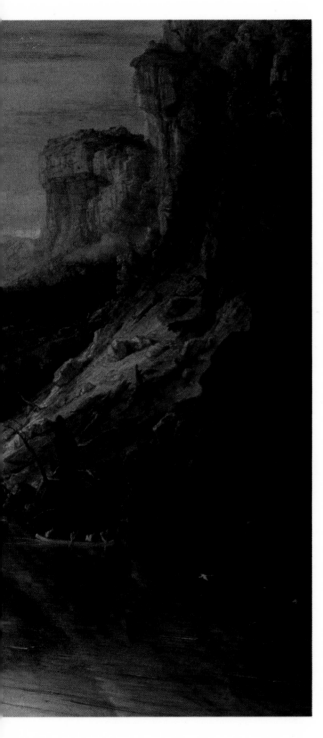

about Verrazano's so-called isthmus, but in England, the theory that "Verrazano's Sea" was an arm of the Pacific continued to stimulate imaginations for many years. As late as 1651 a map of Virginia placed the Pacific a mere 10 days' trek from the head of the James River. Verrazano himself never learned of his error. In 1528, on an expedition to the Caribbean to procure dyewood—and to continue the search for a strait to the Pacific—the navigator was captured by a tribe of cannibalistic Caribs, and was killed and eaten on the beach while his brother and some crewmen watched helplessly from a boat in the surf.

The French did not give up the quest. On April 20, 1534, Jacques Cartier, an expert Breton navigator, left St.-Malo with two 60-ton ships and 61 men. His instructions from Francis I were "to discover certain islands and lands where it is said a great quantity of gold and other precious things are to be found." Cartier's course was nearly due west; 20 days later he raised land at Cape Bonavista, on the east coast of Newfoundland. In the decade since Verrazano's coastal survey, French fishermen had brought back word of a westward-trending water channel north of the Newfoundland fishing grounds. Cartier himself may have made an unofficial exploration of this area earlier. In any case, he apparently accepted Verrazano's conclusion that there was no passage to the Pacific in latitudes south of Newfoundland, for after spending 10 days making repairs and waiting for favorable winds he headed north.

On this initial voyage, which lasted four and a half months, Cartier penetrated the Strait of Belle Isle and methodically charted the vast gulf into which it opened. Intent on getting through to the Eastern Ocean and Cathay, he followed one promising waterway 80 miles, only to have his hopes dashed when Chaleur Bay proved a dead end. By September 5, Cartier was back in St.-Malo, where he immediately began drumming up support for a return journey. Although he had not found a passage this time out, he knew exactly where he was going to pick up the trail.

Cartier's second voyage began on May 19, 1535. He had more than 100 men and three ships—the 120-ton *Grand Hermine*, the 60-ton *Petite Hermine* and the 40-ton pinnace *Emerillon*. This time he also had guides: two young Indians whom Cartier had taken back to France the year before. By September 7 they had brought him to their home village of Stadacona—the site of modern Quebec City—on the great waterway they knew as the Hochelaga and that Cartier called simply La Grande Rivière. (The name St. Lawrence, which Cartier's successors applied to both the gulf and the river, was one he had given to a small, sheltered harbor on the south shore of what is now Quebec province.)

The Indians told the explorer that the river led to a land rich in gold and precious stones—the kingdom of Saguenay. After resting several days at Stadacona and finding a safe anchorage for the two larger ships, Cartier proceeded upriver in the pinnace on September 19. It was a tricky undertaking, for there were rapids, banks of shale covered with boulders, and an ebb current of some five and a half knots. The little ship could make scarcely eight miles a day. On October 2, having come the last 40 miles in the longboats, Cartier reached a well-fortified Indian village at the base of an impressive hill. Cartier called this prominence Mont Réal—a name that would be applied to the city that later grew

around it. He had come nearly 1,000 miles from the Atlantic Ocean in his search for a passage through the continent and for the riches of Saguenay en route. But here the navigator was stymied: Above the village lay impenetrable rapids—"the most impetuous one could possibly see," he reported. (In the next century another French explorer would name these rapids La Chine, an ironic joke implying that this was as close as Cartier ever came to China.) The weather was turning cold, and—according to the Indians—Saguenay was several weeks' journey away. Cartier turned back, mission unaccomplished, and settled down for the winter in the fort his men had erected near Stadacona.

The French were thus the first Europeans to face the debilitating hardships of a northern winter in the New World. For five solid months their ships were locked in ice that was more than two fathoms thick. Scurvy broke out among the Europeans and Indians alike. This disease, first described by Hippocrates in the Fourth Century B.C., is caused by a lack of vitamin C, whose chief dietary source is fresh fruits and vegetables. But the Frenchmen shivering on the banks of the St. Lawrence did not know causes, only effects: Gums rotted, teeth fell out, limbs swelled painfully and an overwhelming lassitude descended. At one point, fewer than a dozen of Cartier's men were in any condition to help their fellows. By the time spring finally freed the ships and Cartier set sail for France, he had buried "25 of the best and most able seamen we had."

Sea monsters believed to inhabit the North Atlantic crowd a 16th Century woodcut. The public so loved to hear and read about the presumed demons of the deep that one returning explorer felt compelled to apologize for his failure to sight monsters during a foray to the New World.

Cartier returned to the St. Lawrence for the third and last time in 1541. The kingdom of Saguenay continued to elude him, and his effort to found a colony failed after one winter, as did another French attempt the next year. Sixty years would pass before France tried again. Eventually, of course, the valley of the St. Lawrence would become the main axis of the French colonial presence in the New World.

England, meanwhile, displayed little exploratory initiative, in part because of a continuing conservatism of geographical thought. Geography, when it was taught at all, remained firmly rooted in the classical, Ptolemaic world; more recent discoveries—including the Cabots' findings—were scarcely acknowledged. The rare Englishman who wished to keep up with contemporary theory was severely handicapped by the dearth of geographical literature on his side of the Channel. Even those in the business of voyaging, wrote one 16th Century chronicler, suffered a "want of skill in Cosmographie, and the Art of Navigation." Unlike Spain, England had no institutions to develop skilled pilots, and it had no tradition of cartography such as had existed in Portugal from the time of Prince Henry the Navigator.

Much of this seemed to change rather abruptly in midcentury, but the seeds of change had been planted some 20 years earlier. Beginning in 1533, King Henry VIII, in defiance of Rome, set out on a path that would lead to the establishment of the Protestant Church of England. That year he divorced his Spanish Queen, Catherine of Aragon, who had been unable to give him a male heir, and married Anne Boleyn. These actions virtually demolished the Anglo-Spanish alliance for the time being— and liberated England's enterprising spirit. By the 1550s, English buccaneers were among those raiding the Spanish Main almost at will, and other merchant-seamen were beginning an active trade with the Barbary States of North Africa for gold and ivory.

In the meantime, a lively cross-pollination was occurring in the once-isolated field of English geographical thought, for religious upheavals on both sides of the Channel had created an itinerant class of Protestant exiles—French Huguenots in the 1540s, English Protestants in the 1540s and 1550s (when there was a brief return of Catholicism to England). Among those who fled to England were French cosmographers and navigators who offered their services to Henry VIII. The maps, charts and manuscripts they brought with them were a revelation to the English. Exiled English Protestants, in turn, immersed themselves in the wealth of geographical literature to be found in such centers as Antwerp and Strasbourg.

Contributing to this nascent fascination with parts unknown was the growing need of English merchants, who had largely saturated their traditional European markets, to find new outlets for their goods, especially English woolens. While ventures in Africa were profitable, there was little call for woolen clothes near the Equator.

Into this welter of restless mercantile, intellectual and maritime energies stepped a brilliant and multifaceted Welshman named John Dee, who returned to England from abroad in 1551. Dee had spent time studying at the University of Louvain under the eminent Flemish mathematician and cosmographer Gemma Phrysius. Most recently, Dee had been in Paris, where he had delivered a series of lectures that greatly impressed several prominent Englishmen then at the court of the French monarch. Over the next three decades, Dee would undertake the technical instruction of an entire generation of English navigators and would exert a powerful influence on the thinking of most of the men who promoted English exploration.

Dee was an unabashed practitioner of astrology and a dabbler in the occult arts of Arab alchemists. These interests made him slightly disreputable in some circles, but his credentials as a mathematician were impeccable, and he counted among his intimate friends such highly regarded mathematicians and cosmographers as Gerard Mercator, Abraham Ortelius and the Portuguese Pedro Nuñez. When he returned to England, he brought not only an extensive library, but a collection of navigational paraphernalia, including the cross-staff—an improved instrument for taking the altitude of a heavenly body to determine latitude—and a globe, made by his old mentor Gemma Phrysius, that showed a wide strait over the top of North America. Dee's own theory of Arctic geography differed slightly from his teacher's: While he believed in the existence of the Northwest Passage, he also believed that a northeastern route to Cathay was feasible.

The latter view had an exceedingly powerful champion in England—John Dudley, Lord Admiral until Henry VIII's death in 1547 and now the Duke of Northumberland. In effect, Northumberland ruled the country for the young and sickly Edward VI. He and a group of about 200 London merchants favored the northeastern route for the pragmatic reason that the presumably civilized inhabitants of northern Asia would be a better market for English woolens than the barbaric natives of North America.

In 1553 the group raised £25,000 and formed what they called the Company of Merchant Adventurers, under a royal charter that awarded them a monopoly on exploration to the north, northeast and northwest. Their first governor was none other than Sebastian Cabot. Northumberland had helped lure the old veteran back to England several years earlier, and the navigator had since invested in a number of trading voyages to Africa. Cabot himself probably would have preferred to lead an expedition to search for the Northwest Passage; he had guarded the details of his youthful attempt throughout his long years in Spain. But the company voted in the end for the route to the northeast, and Cabot set to work organizing a three-ship expedition to this heretofore untried quadrant of exploration.

The expedition left London in May 1553, under the leadership of Sir Hugh Willoughby. Not much is known about Willoughby's previous maritime experience. He had a good record of service on land in England's wars with Scotland, and his appearance was deemed suitably commanding for this important enterprise. Second in command was Richard Chancellor, a professional seaman from Bristol, who was the expedition's chief pilot. His abilities as a mathematician and maker of navigational instruments had earned him the respect of John Dee, who worked with him to prepare the celestial charts and tables that were necessary for the voyage.

Opening moves in an epic quest

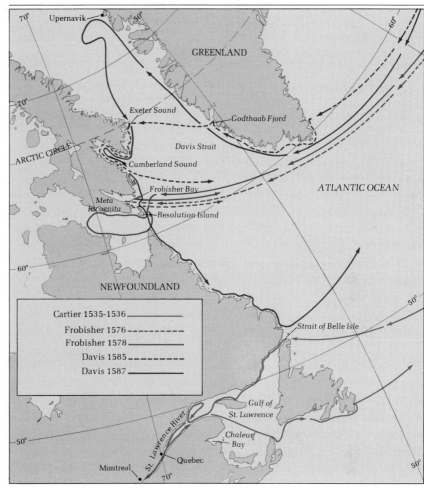

In the 16th Century, mariners seeking a passage to Cathay began to prick the skin of North America. Jacques Cartier found the St. Lawrence seaway, opening up Canada to the French; Martin Frobisher penetrated turbulent Hudson Strait; and John Davis pointed the way toward Baffin Bay, whose western shore held the key to the Northwest Passage.

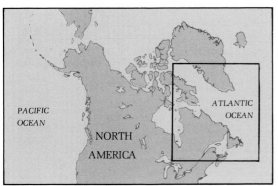

Despite its careful planning, the expedition failed tragically in its primary mission. The ships became separated, and Willoughby, with two of the vessels, went ahead past North Cape. About two weeks later he discovered Novaya Zemlya, the bleak archipelago that forms the western boundary of the Kara Sea. Shortly afterward one of the ships began leaking, and Willoughby turned back. The onset of winter caught the explorers in Lapland. Although the men had more than enough provisions to last until spring, they were not equipped to deal with the cold. The entire company froze to death.

In the meantime, Chancellor, captain of the third ship, had penetrated and begun to explore the White Sea. Here he encountered a boatload of fishermen who informed him—to his great surprise—that he had arrived in the territory of the Russian Czar. None of Sebastian Cabot's instructions had suggested such a possibility. But Chancellor was equal to the unexpected: He went ashore and prevailed upon the reluctant villagers of Archangel to lend him sledges and horses for the rugged 1,000-mile trek to Moscow. The Englishman's arrival there could not have been more timely. Czar Ivan the Terrible had recently broken with the German Hanseatic League, a powerful merchant association that had provided his only link to Europe. When Chancellor made his way home in the summer of 1554, he brought a letter offering the English lucrative trading privileges within the Czar's empire: In exchange for English arms, woolen cloth and other manufactured goods, Russia would supply furs, hemp and tallow.

Such was the promise of the Russian connection that the Muscovy, or Russia, Company, as the Merchant Adventurers soon came to be called, shelved its plans for seeking a passage to Cathay. The company sent Chancellor on a second visit to Ivan to work out details for a treaty. On his journey back to England in 1556, he perished in a shipwreck off the coast of Scotland. An illustrious passenger, the Russian Ambassador, was saved, however, and eventually reached London. He was welcomed with great pomp, and a formal commercial treaty was duly signed by Queen Mary, who had been crowned three years earlier. For the next quarter of a century, while the Muscovy Company followed its mercantile interests through Russia and on into Persia, its monopoly on exploration for a passage to the Orient through the northern part of the globe would lie fallow.

As for the English government, Mary's interests lay closer to home. In her determination to restore England to Catholicism, she had married the Spanish King, Philip II, in 1554, tying England's interests once again to those of Spain and involving the country in war with France. But just four years later, Mary was dead, as was the briefly resuscitated Spanish alliance. Her Protestant half sister, Elizabeth, succeeded to the throne— to find the royal treasury empty. Mary had consistently overspent her revenues by some 40 per cent, badly compounding the debt of £200,000 she had inherited from Edward VI. Moreover, the loss of Calais, England's bridgehead on the European continent for more than two centuries, had undermined the nation's prestige abroad and sapped its pride at home. Elizabeth's first concern was to restore the nation's credit and its self-respect. Speculative voyages of discovery would have to await England's revitalization.

Throughout the early years of Elizabeth's reign, two voices kept up a dogged clamor for ventures to open a route to Cathay—and eventually they found listeners. One voice belonged to John Dee, who had switched his allegiance from the presumptive northeastern passage to the northwestern route featured on the globe of his erstwhile professor, Phrysius. The other belonged to a quintessentially Elizabethan gentleman of Devonshire named Humphrey Gilbert. To be born in Devon was in those days to be a seaman, and Gilbert was, in fact, related to the Hawkinses, Grenvilles and other great seafaring families; Walter Raleigh, at least 10 years his junior, was his half brother. Yet the man himself was little more than an armchair sailor for most of his life. His mark on English exploration would come less from actual voyaging than from a vigorous and unremitting espousal of maritime expansion.

In 1566 Elizabeth turned down a petition from Gilbert to seek the Northwest Passage. Undaunted, Gilbert then wrote a summary of all the arguments for the venture, in hopes of raising support elsewhere. The Muscovy Company, still facing east, was not interested. But Gil-

The frontispiece of The Arte of Navigation, by the 16th Century navigational genius John Dee, depicts Queen Elizabeth steering a ship labeled "Europa," symbolizing Dee's conviction that Britain would establish an empire through supremacy at sea. He urged the country's leading explorers to seek a northwest or a northeast passage to Cathay.

GENERAL AND RARE MEMORIALS
pertayning to the Perfect Arte of
NAVIGATION:

Annexed to the PARADOXAL *Cumpas, in Playne :*
now first published : 24. yeres, after the first
Inuention thereof.

bert's proposal, which circulated in manuscript for 10 years before it was published, was to have a lasting effect on English exploration. His *Discourse of a discoverie for a new passage to Cataia* (Cathay) comprised 10 chapters and 10,000 words. It brought together—without too much scruple about truth—most of the proofs for the existence of such a passage, citing authorities from Plato and Pliny to Peter Martyr, the Spanish chronicler of exploration. To discredit promoters of a northeast passage, Gilbert devoted three chapters and some tenuous arguments (mostly having to do with fish and unicorns) to demonstrate that it was not navigable. Finally, he listed the prizes that awaited the discoverer: an unquenchable market for exports, the elimination of Spanish and Portuguese middlemen, supplies of gold, silk, velvet and spices, an incentive to build a great navy and the palpable certainty of becoming the reigning nation of the world.

Another of Gilbert's arguments in favor of this venture was slightly ahead of its time: "Also we might inhabit some part of those countries," he wrote, "and settle there such needy people of our country, which now trouble the commonwealth, and through want here at home are inforced to commit outrageous offences, whereby they are dayly consumed with the gallows." Thus was England's far-flung empire foreshadowed.

In 1574 Gilbert again petitioned the Queen, and again he was refused. But another man—assisted in courtly intrigue by John Dee and some of the Queen's closest advisers, including Sir Francis Walsingham—soon thereafter succeeded where Gilbert had failed. Backed by a letter from the Privy Council, a Yorkshire sea captain named Martin Frobisher persuaded the obstinate Muscovy Company to relinquish to a new Company of Cathay its long-unused monopoly on northern exploration. Unpredictable Elizabeth gave her blessing. And money to renew the quest was provided by a prosperous merchant and shipowner, Michael Lok.

Frobisher—blond, blue-eyed, and of legendary strength and courage—was a veteran of several sea journeys to the west of Africa, and of several of those acts of piracy against the Spanish at which the Queen (provided official encouragement was never acknowledged) was happy to wink. Virtually illiterate, he had gained his interest in the search directly from Gilbert, whom he had met while both were fighting rebels in Ireland in the 1560s.

The mariner made no pretense of being cleverer than he was. Despite intensive instruction by Dee in the use of the best navigational instruments available—including the cross-staff Dee had brought back from the Netherlands—Frobisher confessed in a letter that very little remained in his head. Maps and charts were easier, and the expedition had them in abundance. But there was one item that Frobisher would have been better off without—the so-called Zeno map *(page 30)*, which purported to show North Atlantic islands visited by a pair of 14th Century Venetians named Nicolò and Antonio Zeno. It misled Frobisher —and, because respected geographers like Mercator and Ortelius accepted it as accurate, it would continue to confuse other navigators for nearly two centuries.

Frobisher set off in June 1576 with provisions for 12 months. There were three ships: the *Michael* and the *Gabriel*—both small barks of

Martin Frobisher, a burly adventurer who served Queen Elizabeth in activities as diversified as fighting rebels in Ireland and preying on Spanish treasure ships, is portrayed with his pistol at the ready. In 1576 he sailed in search of the Northwest Passage, returned with samples of what some believed to be gold ore and set off a rush to the Arctic.

under 30 tons, with crews of about 18 apiece—and, for probing shallows, a seven-ton pinnace with a crew of four. The vessels sailed up the east coast of England, passed between the Orkney and the Shetland Islands and then struck out westward into the North Atlantic. At the end of June, when they were hardly out of sight of the Shetlands, the first of many misfortunes occurred. A gale blew up and raged for eight days. At the end of it, the pinnace had disappeared. "Neither it nor its crew was ever seen again," wrote George Best, Frobisher's companion and chronicler of the voyage.

On July 11 the voyagers glimpsed the southern coast of Greenland—wrongly identified on the Zeno map as a separate island called Frisland. Awed by the "marvellous abundance of monstrous great islands of ice which lay driving all along the coast thereof," Best wrote, and frustrated by this same ice in all attempts to reach the shore, they continued on their way. Soon, however, the little flotilla was reduced to one. "Mistrusting the matter," Best recorded, the crew of the *Michael* "conveyed themselves privilie away" and returned to London. There—presumably to cover their own cowardice—they spread the canard that Frobisher and the *Gabriel* were lost.

The master of the *Gabriel* was very much alive; indeed he seemed indomitable. When another great storm laid the ship on her beam-ends and began to fill her with water, Frobisher himself braved the wind and seas to cast off lines and braces; then he ordered the mizzenmast hacked off—and the little bark righted.

In late July the explorers sighted what the Zeno map indicated was Greenland. Their landfall was actually a little island off the southern tip of what would later be named Baffin Island, which forms the main eastern boundary of the Canadian Arctic. Frobisher named his landfall Queen Elizabeth's Foreland; it is now called Resolution Island.

He steered north and soon found an inlet—or, as George Best put it, "a great gutte, bay or passage, dividing as it were two mayne lands or continents asunder." For several days Frobisher sailed the *Gabriel* into this "gutte." One hundred and fifty miles later, as the lands he took to be the Asian and American continents slid past on either side and the waters ahead showed no obstacle, Frobisher concluded that he had found what he sought: the Northwest Passage. Mindful of Ferdinand Magellan's famous straits at the southern extremity of the New World land mass, he gave the waterway the proprietary name of Frobisher's Straits. Had he sailed 50 miles farther, he would have discovered that his "straits" were merely a bight poking deep into Baffin Island.

For the moment, however, the Yorkshireman decided to take stock of this region. In the course of peregrinations ashore, Best wrote, Frobisher noted the remains of fires and other signs that the land was inhabited. Then a "mighty deere"—probably a musk ox—"ranne at him and hardly he escaped with his life." From the top of a hill, he spied "a number of small things fleeting in the sea afarre off," which he took to be porpoises or seals. "But coming nearer, he discovered them to be men in small boates made of leather."

In the next century, white men would give the human inhabitants of these icy wastes the name Eskimo—a corruption of an Indian word

A mythic rendition of the North Atlantic

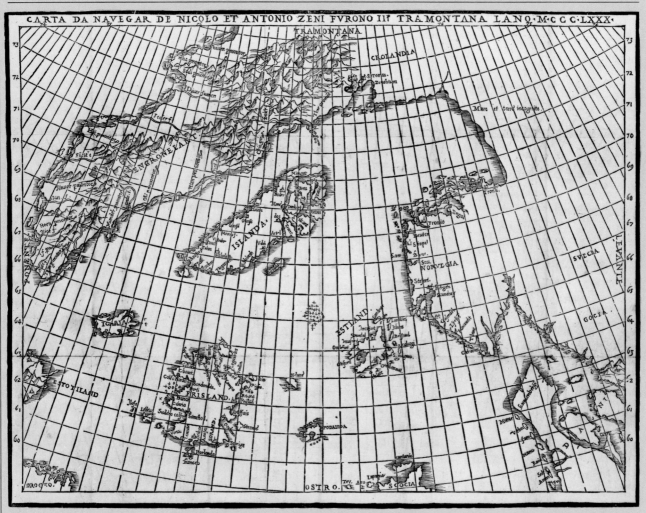

On the Zeno map, nonexistent isles dot the Atlantic, and Greenland (called Engronelant) is shown as a peninsula of Europe.

As Martin Frobisher voyaged across the Atlantic to find a passage to Cathay, he relied on the map pictured above, never guessing that it contained more false information than true. No fewer than five of the land masses that are depicted here—Estland, Frisland, Icaria, Estotiland and Drogeo—are fictitious, evidently created as part of a bold bid for empire.

The map was published in 1558 by a Venetian named Nicolò Zeno, and it was accompanied by fragments of letters that two of his ancestors, an earlier Nicolò Zeno and his brother Antonio, had allegedly written 150 years earlier. According to the letters, the venturesome brothers had been shipwrecked on a North Atlantic island called Frisland in 1380. There they met a prince named Zichmni, who directed them to wondrous countries—one where gold was as common as fish (Estotiland), another inhabited by naked and menacing cannibals (Drogeo), and yet another that boasted a church honoring Saint Thomas and a hill that spewed fire (Engronelant).

When the map and accompanying text appeared, Venetians reacted with understandable acclaim: If Estotiland were the New World, as its location seemed to indicate, the Zeno brothers had reached it well ahead of Christopher Columbus. Unfortunately for Venetian hopes, Spain and other claimants to the Americas dismissed the work as a fraud. Several distinguished geographers, however, accepted its vision of the North Atlantic as fact. Thus, when Frobisher came upon Greenland, he took it to be the mythical Frisland. And the coast he believed to be Greenland actually was Baffin Island, 800 miles farther west. More than a century would elapse before these errors were corrected and Zeno's map consigned to cartographic oblivion.

for them. Frobisher called them "savages" or, in a more kindly vein, "countrey people." His sailing master, Christopher Hall, observed that they resembled "Tartars, with long blacke haire, broad faces and flatte noses." The women tattooed and painted blue streaks on their cheeks and around their eyes.

Aboard the *Gabriel*, a jovial dispensing of trinkets soon gave place to doubt and disaster. Five of Frobisher's men, told to row one of the Eskimos back to shore, disobeyed strict orders to return to the ship immediately. Instead, they went to do a little trading. The men—and the ship's only boat—were never seen again.

Frobisher resolved to take hostages to exchange for his men, but the Eskimos kept out of reach for several days. Finally he succeeded in luring one of them within range by tinkling a bell; the burly Frobisher "caught the man fast," Best reported, and "plucked him with maine force boate and al into his bark out of the sea." The prisoner, "for very choller and disdaine," bit his tongue in two. An attempt was made to barter for the return of the five Englishmen, but without success. Now Frobisher sent his men ashore with orders to gather whatever souvenirs they could find (since they had no boat, Best wrote, they went "by any possible means"—presumably meaning that they swam). The group picked up odds and ends—flowers, grass and sticks—and returned safely to the ship. Then, with favorable but stormy winds, the *Gabriel* beat a path for England.

One maimed Eskimo was hardly a triumphant prize to show when the depleted crew reached London on October 9. Yet Frobisher was celebrated for "his great and notable attempt," wrote Best, "but especially famous for the great hope he brought of the passage to Cataya." No one doubted he had charted the opening of the long-hidden passage. While the captured Eskimo lived—which was not long, since he had none of the immunities needed to survive in the white man's world—he and his kayak were objects of intense curiosity to Londoners. Yet the greatest excitement of all was stirred by one of the souvenirs a sailor had brought back—a piece of black stone, "which by the weight seemed to be some kind of metal or mineral," Best said. Thrown by chance on a fire, the stone "glistered with a bright marquesset of golde." Though most assayers were skeptical, one was found who was prepared to assert that the glitter was gold indeed.

There was no doubt now about a return voyage. This new expedition's sole purpose was to mine ore; searching for a passage to Cathay was not part of Frobisher's orders. The Queen herself provided a ship, the 200-ton *Aid*, to escort the *Gabriel* and *Michael*, and allowed Frobisher to kiss her hand before his departure in late May of 1577. Soon he was again in sight of Greenland, and of icebergs up to half a mile in circumference.

By July he had found the site from which the shining rock had been extracted. The next six weeks were eventful. One stormy day, the master of the *Michael* was washed overboard and drowned. On a less tragic occasion, the Englishmen spied what they called a "sea unicorne," a four-yard-long fish embedded in ice and displaying "a horne of two yardes long growing out of the snoute or nostrels." (It was, in fact, the Arctic cetacean now called a narwhal.) During this time, relations with the Eskimos varied—not surprisingly, since the Englishmen wanted specimens to take home for exhibit. At one point, a bloody battle broke out; one sailor was wounded and six Eskimos killed.

But the Englishmen devoted most of their energies to digging up the scattered deposits of alleged gold, and when they departed for home they had a cargo of 200 tons. Back in England, assayers continued to test the rock and to argue over their findings. Although doubters were numerous, they were not persuasive enough to deflate what had now become a market boom.

In 1578 Frobisher mounted a third expedition with investments totalling £6,952, more than half of it from the Queen. Fifteen ships were fitted out to retrieve maximum quantities of the rock, and the company was large enough so that about 100 men could be left behind to start England's first colony—a mining camp. On this journey, whose outward route varied little from that of the other two, the weather played a decidedly malevolent role.

For two weeks after the Englishmen sighted Baffin Island, ice and storms prevented the ships from getting in to shore. It was only with extreme difficulty that Frobisher managed to keep the fleet together. As it was, the ship that was carrying supplies and building timbers for the intended colony was sunk by an iceberg, although all hands were saved. When the storms abated, Frobisher and his fleet found themselves in what they thought was Frobisher's Straits. But as Frobisher followed the channel westward, he realized he was in unfamiliar waters. For several days he sailed on, and eventually he came to the conclusion that these "Mistaken Straits," as he called them, were more than likely the true passage to Cathay (he was actually in Hudson Strait, first seen by Sebastian Cabot 69 years earlier). But now—to his chagrin, for he would have liked to explore farther—he had orders to mine gold. He turned the fleet around. Getting out of the strait was harder than getting in. Frobisher battled head winds and, at the mouth—in the gap between Resolution Island and Labrador—a turbulent riptide. Eventually he made it back to Meta Incognita, as the Queen had dubbed the site of his presumptive gold mine on Baffin Island.

So extreme was the weather that Frobisher was hard put to carry out his instructions. Snowstorms alternated with debilitating heat, and mutinous murmurs began to circulate among the crew. Finally, the fleet left for home at the beginning of September. No one stayed to winter over.

A much more serious setback awaited Frobisher in England. He learned that the dithering assayers had at last reached a definite verdict. The traces of metal in his huge trophy of stone were nothing but mica and iron pyrites, with no intrinsic value. The harvest of three costly and courageous voyages was subsequently used to repair roads in Kent.

Frobisher lived to distinguish himself in the harassment of the Spanish Armada, and to receive a knighthood from the Queen. But his exploring days were over. His three voyages had fired the hope for a northwestern route to the Orient for three years running, but the fiasco of the false gold had in the end overshadowed the expedition's original purpose and served to quash interest in further efforts for some time. Too many important people—including the Queen—had lost money on the venture;

Amid the floes of a Baffin Island bay, Frobisher's crew repels an Eskimo attack. The battle erupted after the explorers tried to find five of their fellows who had been captured on a previous visit to the bay. This encounter left one Englishman wounded and half a dozen Eskimos dead.

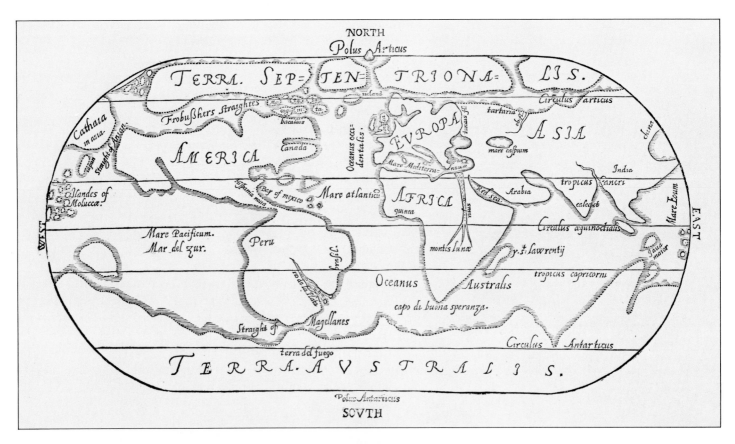

A map published in 1578 by Martin Frobisher's shipmate George Best shows a direct route from Europe to the Orient by way of "straightes" across the top of North America. A voyage to Cathay, said Best, "was not onely possible by the Northwest," but "easie to bee performed."

too many people soon vanished from the scene. The principal backer, Michael Lok, was to spend several years in debtor's prison for bankruptcy brought on by the disaster. Humphrey Gilbert, that persistent champion of the Northwest Passage, transferred his passion to founding an English colony in the New World, and in 1583, on his way back from a colonizing effort, was lost at sea.

But Gilbert's younger brother, Adrian, kept the family interest in voyaging alive, and in 1585 he obtained permission from the Queen to resume the search for Cathay. Adrian Gilbert was joined in the venture by Sir Francis Walsingham, who had not lost faith in spite of his losses in the Frobisher enterprise. Other backers included merchants from the Devon port of Exeter and a wealthy London businessman named William Sanderson. Even John Dee, instructor of northern navigators from Willoughby to Frobisher, was a member of the company for a while—until he took it into his head, following a series of séances, that the others were turning against him. He decamped for the Continent, and his academic reputation never recovered. Command of the expedition was given to a native of Devonshire and lifelong friend of Humphrey and Adrian Gilbert, John Davis.

In June of that year Davis set off in the 50-ton *Sunshine*, with 35 men, accompanied by the 35-ton *Moonshine* with a crew of 19. The voyage was chronicled by John Janes, Sanderson's nephew, who sailed as clerk and supercargo. On July 19, having been delayed for 12 days at the Scilly Islands by contrary winds, Davis' ships encountered thick fog and a strong north-running tide. When the weather cleared the next day, the men found themselves near a coast "which was the most deformed rocky and mountainous land that we ever saw," Janes wrote, "and the shore beset with ice a league off into the sea, making such irksome noise as that it seemed to be the sure pattern of desolation." Again because of the Zeno map, Davis did not recognize that this was the southeast coast of Greenland. He named it the "Land of Desolation."

After rounding the tip of Greenland, he sailed 400 miles up its west coast to an inlet he called Gilbert's Sound, after Sir Humphrey (it is now Godthaab Fjord). There, freedom from ice finally allowed him to anchor close to shore. Eskimos appeared and, with marvelous inspiration, the captain of the *Moonshine* ordered the ship's musicians to strike up a tune. The Eskimos so enjoyed the sailors' dancing that three times as many natives showed up the next day. Trading was lively. "They are a very tractable people," Janes observed, "and easy to be brought to any civility or good order."

On August 1, the two barks sailed with a northeast wind across the strait that now bears Davis' name, to an inlet on Baffin Island at latitude 66° 40′ that he named Exeter Sound. Farther south, he came on a broad opening to the west, which immediately raised hopes that this was the sought-for passage. He named it Cumberland Sound after one of the investors in the voyage. After sailing up it for some 180 miles, and finding that the water was deeper than his sounding line could measure, Davis was increasingly persuaded that he had indeed found the way to Cathay. There were other signs that lent support to this view: Whales were seen to the west, after none had been seen on the open sea, and the tides were fast and strong. But the truth is that neither Davis nor his contemporaries, nor any of the explorers who were to follow him during the next half century, knew enough about currents (which can often be set up by Atlantic tides) or whales (which regularly swim into blind bays in search of food), or geology or geography to make informed guesses about their prospects.

In any event, the wind soon shifted to the northwest, and Davis elected to head for home. The season was getting on, and their supplies would not have lasted a wintering over. But the navigator believed, as he wrote to Walsingham soon after his return, that "the northwest passage is a matter nothing doubtful, but at any time almost to be passed, the sea navigable, void of ice, the air tolerable, and the waters very deep." Six months later, inspired by Davis' optimism, his backers had raised funds and provided ships for a second voyage.

In addition to the *Sunshine* and the *Moonshine*, Davis now had the 120-ton *Mermaid* and the 10-ton pinnace *North Star* at his command. Davis' hopes focused on the most northerly latitudes, for he held to a popular theory that, because the Arctic sun did not set for several months of the year, the waters around the Pole were free of ice and would provide the shortest navigable route to the east. He sent the *Sunshine* and the *North Star* to explore the east coast of Greenland, while he continued with the other two vessels up Davis Strait to Gilbert's Sound. Here they met Eskimos again. Sometimes as many as 100 kayaks would gather near the ships, bringing skins, deer and fish to barter for trinkets. Wrestling contests were held, and the men of Devonshire, though judged prodigious wrestlers at home, came out second best. Familiarity began to breed a form of contempt, however, for the Eskimos now began to steal iron cables, oars and finally an anchor.

Leaving Gilbert's Sound, Davis tried to sail farther north, but he found ice blocking the sea at 63° N., whereas the year before the way had been clear. Now men began to fall sick and talk of going home. Davis put those who were ill aboard the *Mermaid* since she was "not so convenient and nimble as a smaller bark," he wrote later, and sent them back to England. He continued on in the *Moonshine* with a picked crew.

After the *Mermaid's* departure, Davis crossed the strait to Baffin Island. Now something inexplicable happened. Although he apparently made roughly the same landfalls as on his first journey, Davis seems not to have recognized the opening to Cumberland Sound when he crossed it. Instead, he continued to sail south as far as the coast of Labrador, missing both Frobisher's Straits and the promise of Frobisher's "Mistaken Straits." The *Moonshine* coasted all the way to 54° 30', dropping anchor from time to time to fish. At one point his men were attacked by "the brutish people of this country," as Davis called them. Two of his seamen were killed and three wounded. Finally, on September 11, the expedition headed home.

The voyage, to all outward appearances, had been a total failure. Davis had neither followed through on his original hunch nor discovered any other likely opening. The two ships he had sent up the east coast of Greenland had had no better luck in finding a passage, and one, the little *North Star*, had been lost on the journey home. Despite the poor showing, Davis remained supremely confident that the passage was there, and—as he declared in his report to William Sanderson—he was ready to sell his family estate to raise funds in order to "see an end of these businesses." The Exeter merchants were not of a mind to throw more money down this rathole of a venture, but Sanderson and his London friends anted up again—although they hedged their bet a little by arranging to have some commercial fishing done on the side.

Davis' third expedition left on May 19, 1587. This time he had three vessels: the tried-and-true *Sunshine*, the Dartmouth-based *Elizabeth* and a clinker-built pinnace out of London named the *Ellen*. Davis was leery of taking a "clincher" like the *Ellen* on such a long journey, but in the end—as the *Sunshine* turned leaky and both her crew and that of the *Elizabeth* elected to go fishing rather than exploring—the *Ellen* carried him on his most important voyage yet.

By June 30, still believing in the possibility of clear water near the Pole, Davis had sailed up Davis Strait to 72° 12'. The sea was indeed clear ahead of him, and in high spirits he named a prominent headland on the Greenland coast Sanderson's Hope after his most loyal backer. The promontory, near the site of the community of Upernavik, would be a noted landmark for the host of explorers who followed. But Davis was prevented from going farther north by head winds, so he sailed west—only to run into an enormous pack of ice. He had to turn southward to get past it. At one point, thinking he spied a channel and clear water beyond, he entered the pack, only to be surrounded and nearly crushed by monstrous icebergs. The escape was a narrow one.

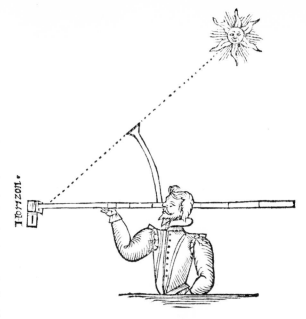

Using a navigational device called a backstaff, a seaman adjusts an arclike armature until it casts a shadow on the end of the instrument; the armature measured the angle of the sun above the horizon, which in turn indicated the ship's latitude. The backstaff, invented in the late 16th Century by explorer John Davis, remained in use for 200 years.

On July 19, he reached the east coast of Baffin Island at Exeter Sound, and this time, as he coasted south, he found the entrance to Cumberland Sound. Ten days later, he had sailed to the end of the sound and out again, thus eliminating it as a route to the Orient.

Continuing to the south, Davis passed an inlet that he named after John, Baron Lumley, one of Elizabeth's courtiers. It was, in fact, Frobisher's Straits (now Bay), but because of the confusion caused by Frobisher's charting—based on the Zeno vision of geography—Davis did not recognize it: Frobisher, and some map makers, had placed the inlet on Greenland. Davis' own navigation—aided by a modified back-staff of his own invention (opposite)—was the most accurate so far. He was hampered, as all navigators would be for two centuries more, by the lack of an accurate seagoing timepiece for the calculation of longitude, but subsequent Arctic explorers would marvel at the remarkable precision of his reported latitudes.

The next day the little Ellen sailed across the mouth of "another very great inlet, whose south limit at this present we saw not," Davis wrote in his log. "To our great admiration, we saw the sea falling down into the gulfe with a mighty overfal, and roring, and with divers circular motions like whirlpools." Perhaps Davis would have investigated Frobisher's "Mistaken Straits" if he had realized where he was, but ice was being driven out of its mouth at such a rate that the Ellen was in danger of swamping as she tried to get across. After a brief coasting of Labrador, Davis headed home on August 15, where he found the Sunshine and the Elizabeth had already returned with great hauls of fish.

Davis, like Frobisher, had failed in three attempts to find a passage through America to Cathay. Yet he never doubted that it was there. "I have been in 73°, finding the sea all open, and forty leagues between land and land," he wrote Sanderson. "The passage is most probable, the execution easy." The following year, however, all exploration was suspended by the outbreak of open war with Spain and Portugal, both ruled by His Catholic Majesty Philip II. Shaping a mighty blow against Protestant heresy, Philip dispatched the Armada northward to England, only to see the prodigious fleet shattered by English cannon and savage storms.

The defeat of the Armada signaled the end of one era and the beginning of another. Although Spain and Portugal regarded the setback as temporary, they would never regain their former dominance of the sea. Soon both English and Dutch vessels began sailing around Africa's Cape of Good Hope to exchange European manufactures for the riches of the Orient—a trade that had been in the hands of the Portuguese for almost a century. Other Dutch and English mariners voyaged around Cape Horn and threatened Spain's traditional hegemony in the Pacific.

But the boldest commercial dream of all, England's vision of a shortcut to Cathay across the top of America, remained just that. Despite Davis' assessment of the opening of the route as "easy," the Arctic Ocean pushed out frigid currents and buffeting gales, mantling the sea with a treacherous carpet of floes and pack ice to forestall even the most intrepid explorers. For the time being, the Northwest Passage remained firmly locked.

A harrowing probe to the northeast

In 1596, when most English explorers believed the only practical short route to the Orient lay to the northwest, a stubborn Dutch navigator named Willem Barents embarked on the last of three attempts to map a northeast passage over the top of Europe and Asia.

The effort cost Barents his life, but a dozen survivors returned to Amsterdam 17 months later. The journal of one of them, which was published in 1599 with these engravings, told a tale of mishaps, frustration and extraordinary human resilience during a winter spent only 950 miles from the Pole.

The expedition began well enough: Sailing his two ships into uncharted waters north of Norway, Barents discovered Bear Island *(below)* and Spitsbergen. However, an argument over where to head next caused the ships to part company. One briefly probed to the northeast before returning to Holland. Barents steered the other eastward across the sea that now bears his name. He made landfall at Novaya Zemlya, a 600-mile-long archipelago separating the Barents Sea from the ice-clogged Kara Sea.

Not far from the northern tip of Novaya Zemlya, ice trapped Barents' ship and inflicted grave damage. The explorers built a sturdy wooden shelter on the shore, but two of the 17 men died of scurvy during the winter—a time, reported sailor Gerrit de Veer in his journal, of "great cold, poverty, misery and grief." Three more, including Barents, succumbed in June and July during a desperate 80-day voyage in small boats to a Dutch trading post on the Russian mainland.

Despite Barents' failure, explorers continued to search for a northeast passage in sailing ships—with no better luck. But the dream would finally be realized in 1879, when a steam-powered whaler carried Swedish explorer Nils Adolf Erik Nordenskjöld over the entire 6,400 miles from the Norwegian Sea through Bering Strait.

Beneath three suns—the two small ones are refracted images called sundogs—Barents' men slay a polar bear near Bear Island.

Clinging desperately to the side of their ice-beset ship in a Novaya Zemlya harbor, three crewmen escape from a floe that began to crack beneath them as they tried to chop open a passage. When the wind rose, ice was driven against the ship with such force that the rudder was smashed.

Battered by floating ice, some "in great heaps, as big as the salt hills that are in Spain," the ship is heaved upward as several crewmen flee with a small boat (left) while others hoist the flags as a distress signal to the landing party at right. Fearing that the vessel would be crushed, the crew voted to spend the winter ashore.

Crewmen use improvised sledges to haul trimmed driftwood to the site of their winter home. Construction of the shelter was impeded by the death of the ship's carpenter and by Arctic storms so fierce that, as de Veer wrote, "we could hardly go against the wind, and a man could hardly draw his breath."

A cutaway view of the 20-by-32-foot house reveals shelflike bunks, a central fireplace and a bath fashioned from a wine cask. A sick man lies close to the fire, while another occupant (background, right) admires the only luxury—a chiming clock that soon succumbed to the cold.

In this composite illustration, Barents' crewmen shoot and then gleefully skin a polar bear that yielded 100 pounds of tallow for their lamps. Nearby, another man sets a weighted trap for Arctic foxes. A lookout surveys the scene from his post at the top of the chimney, which also served as an entrance when snow and ice blocked the doors.

In late May of 1597, as the ice begins to break up, the Dutch prepare one of their boats for the long voyage south by building up the sides with planks stripped from their abandoned ship. Polar bears often approached the party—"as if they had smelled that we would be gone," wrote de Veer, "and that therefore they desired to taste a piece of some of us."

The sailors load their two boats with the remaining provisions—and also with most of the wool, linen and velvet that they had intended to sell in the Orient. A week after they headed south, Barents died—evidently of scurvy—and was buried on the shore of Novaya Zemlya.

A herd of walruses reacts with alarm
as the boats sail by. In the background are
Russian fishermen, who were actually
encountered several days later. Another
month of voyaging brought the
explorers to a Dutch trading post, 1,600
miles from their starting point, and
there they boarded a ship bound for home.

Chapter 2

Siren song of the northern seas

though the English navy and autumn gales all but obliterated the Spanish Armada in 1588, the war with Spain dragged on for another 15 years. In between his assignments on the high seas, John Davis diligently nursed the flickering interest in discovering a northern passage to Cathay. He collaborated with an English mathematician named Emery Molyneaux to fashion a globe that incorporated his discoveries (page 48), and he wrote books.

In *The Seamans Secrets*, published in 1594, Davis explained the fine points of navigation—devoting a chapter to the use of the globe, which he considered "the most rare and excellent" of all instruments—and declared with justifiable pride that, in the matter of seamanship, the English "are not to be matched by any nation of the earth." Hot on the heels of *The Seamans Secrets* came *The Worldes Hydrographical Discription*—a direct appeal to the Privy Council, rather in the same vein as Humphrey Gilbert's *Discourse* of 30 years before, but based on considerably more personal experience. Davis set forth the case for the existence of a northwest passage, lamenting the fact that the war and the death of Secretary Walsingham, his most influential sponsor, had combined to prevent him from continuing his exploration of the promising waters to the north of Davis Strait.

Unhappily for John Davis, English merchant-adventurers were willing to consider only sure investments while the war persisted. The tireless navigator, now approaching his mid-fifties, found himself employed instead on voyages to open up trade with the Far East via the Cape of Good Hope (both the English and the Dutch had managed to get hold of priceless Spanish and Portuguese charts to show the way). On his third such voyage his ship was attacked by Japanese pirates, and Davis succumbed to knife wounds received in the battle. But the clues he left behind in his writings and on the Molyneaux globe would ignite a concentrated search for the Northwest Passage in the first three decades of the 17th Century.

Although the English and Dutch now had a direct link with the Orient, the pressure for a northern connection was greater than ever. Their two trading arms—the English East India Company, chartered in 1600, and its Dutch counterpart, born two years later—soon developed a cutthroat rivalry in the commercial arena. Finding a shorter route to the wealth of the Indies would be a tremendous coup.

In May 1602—as the war with Spain at last showed signs of ending—the English East India Company dispatched George Waymouth with two ships, the 50-ton *Discovery* and the 40-ton *Godspeed*, to pick up where Davis had left off. Waymouth's instructions were to make for Davis Strait "and soe forward by the norwest to the kingdomes of Cataya or China, or the backe side of America." He was also instructed to spend at least a year in the attempt. As it happened, Waymouth was back in three months, the victim of a mutiny. In his vivid but somewhat vague account of the journey, Waymouth reported that he had entered an inlet at 61°40′N. and had sailed "one hundred leagues west and by south." Another voyage to explore this intriguing waterway was contemplated, but the East India Company apparently decided that

Flying the twin lions of Amsterdam from her foremast and the initials of the Dutch East India Company at her stern, a full-sized replica of Henry Hudson's ship, the Half Moon, sails up the Hudson River in 1909 in commemoration of the 300th anniversary of the exploration of that waterway. Although the river failed to provide a passage to the Orient, Hudson's enthusiastic reports persuaded the Dutch to colonize its fertile valley.

the route around the Cape of Good Hope was more practical than any possible Arctic passage.

Now the Muscovy Company, which had paid no attention to the Arctic for half a century, displayed a revived interest in searching for the shortcut to Cathay. In 1607 and again in 1608—still harboring a belief that the likeliest route lay to the north or the northeast rather than across the Atlantic—the company engaged Captain Henry Hudson to command expeditions into those waters. Of Hudson's life up to that time, little is known: He had a wife and three sons, he seems to have come from a family that had nautical connections, and he was now about 40 years old. Although he emerges from obscurity, it is probable that he was a mariner of some experience: Some accounts suggest that he may have sailed with John Davis, and three nations would compete for his services over the next three years. In any event, both of his efforts to find a northeast passage were failures, although his report of a Spitsbergen bay that teemed with whales soon launched a highly profitable industry. Upon returning from his second Arctic voyage, Hudson was eager to try the northwestern Atlantic. But the Muscovy Company had lost its enthusiasm for the project.

Enter the Dutch East India Company, which had been keeping a weather eye on Hudson's activities. After some tricky negotiating—during which France nearly enticed him away—Hudson was persuaded to conduct a return expedition to the Russian Arctic on behalf of the merchants of the Netherlands. For his part, the English captain appears to have been somewhat less than honest in his dealings with his new sponsors. He must have believed that his commission was impossible to fulfill, since he had twice tried and failed. Moreover, his head was dancing with details of the possibilities that beckoned from the other side of the Atlantic.

Hudson had pored over accounts of both Davis' and Waymouth's voyages, and he was utterly fascinated by the great, seething inlet Davis had described as a "furious overfal" (it was so named on the Molyneaux globe). This "overfal" and the entrance to Waymouth's promising inlet appeared to be one and the same. Hudson had also recently received tantalizing information from his friend Captain John Smith, who was in the nascent English colony of Virginia. Smith's letters and maps pointed to a supposed passage somewhere to the north of the colony—probably based on confused Indian accounts of the Great Lakes and on the 85-year-old misconception of "Verrazano's Sea." Hudson's Dutch employers, however, were insistent that he try the northeast once again, and northeast is where he went. But he took Smith's letters and Waymouth's journals with him.

Hudson sailed from Amsterdam in April 1609, in the 80-ton bark *Half Moon*. His mixed crew of about 18 Dutch and English seamen included a hard-bitten sailor named Robert Juet, whose journal is the source of most of what is known about Hudson's third voyage. Juet, now in his fifties, had served as Hudson's first mate the year before. At that time the captain had described him as "filled with mean tempers," and had found him—at best—only grudgingly cooperative. Why Hudson continued to select him for his expeditions is a question no one has been able

As a token of their friendly intentions, Henry Hudson and his crew present beads to inquisitive Indians they met along the Hudson River in 1609. In spite of a few bloody skirmishes, the Indians usually responded cordially to the white strangers, and willingly traded fresh game, fruit and furs for almost any European trinket.

to answer. Perhaps he deemed Juet's experience valuable enough to offset his petty and jealous behavior. If so, it was a judgment Hudson would live to regret.

Early in May the *Half Moon* rounded Norway's North Cape, according to instructions. But shortly after this, mutiny broke out. Conditions that season were appalling: Gales raged, and thick ice often had to be broken off the ropes to allow them to move freely through the pulleys. Many of the Dutch seamen were accustomed to the warmer air along the Cape route and refused to go any farther in a direction that was plainly so inimical to life. Hudson, who was convinced by now that the only northern passage must lie somewhere in the New World, was probably less upset by the mutiny than another captain might have been; indeed, some have suspected that he was a party to the plot. At any rate, he yielded swiftly. But he offered the crew a choice: to head directly for Davis' "furious overfal," or to search for the passage to Cathay in latitudes south of the St. Lawrence and north of Smith's Virginia colony. With Smith's papers to tempt him—and warmer climates to tempt his men—Hudson shaped a course for the west, in direct disobedience of the orders he had received from his employers.

In mid-July, Hudson and the *Half Moon* anchored off the American shore, probably in what is now Penobscot Bay, Maine. They lingered there for about a week, making repairs, replenishing their water supply, and fishing for halibut and lobster. Friendly Indians paddled out to the ship in canoes and readily bartered tobacco and skins for cheap trinkets. On July 24, Hudson's men repaid this openhandedness with treachery—stealing a canoe and ransacking the village. It is not clear whether Hudson condoned this action, but even if he did not, he failed to punish the men who carried it out. The *Half Moon* left Maine before dawn the next morning.

Hudson now coasted southwest, to within reach of Jamestown. But—perhaps because he was flying Dutch colors—he did not stop to visit Captain Smith. Instead, he continued south, probably as far as Cape Hatteras, before turning back to the north for a closer reconnaissance of the coastline where the passage to the Pacific was supposed to be. Chesapeake and Delaware Bays proved disappointing, but following Verrazano, Hudson made a deeper probe of what would be named New York Harbor and the Hudson River.

The inland journey took him some 150 miles up the river, into the shadow of the Adirondack Mountains and, although he was unaware of it, within 100 miles of where the French explorer Samuel de Champlain was then campaigning with the Algonquin Indians against the Iroquois. Hudson's relations with the various Indians he encountered were less clear-cut. He wooed and cheated them alternately, sometimes graciously accepting their hospitality and bartering red cloaks for furs, sometimes taking what he wanted by violence or guile. But the Indians, too, were inconsistent and nervously unpredictable. Early on, possibly in revenge for some affront, Indians attacked five crewmen who were exploring in the ship's boat, and killed one with arrows. But farther up the river, they treated Hudson with generous deference. "The natives are a very good people," Hudson wrote later of a visit to one village, "for

when they saw I would not remain, they supposed that I was afraid of their bows, and taking their arrows, they broke them in pieces, and threw them into the fire."

Near the site of present-day Albany the river became too narrow and shallow to sustain any of Hudson's hopes, and he returned downstream. Two months of patient exploration had persuaded him that this stretch of the coast offered no passage through. There was one remaining possibility— Davis' "furious overfal," far to the north of Newfoundland. It was late September, too late to make an attempt this year. But plans for a return expedition were uppermost in Hudson's mind as he set off to report to the Dutch East India Company on a mission they had never asked him to undertake.

He never reached them. The *Half Moon* docked at Dartmouth, in Devonshire, on November 7, 1609. From here Hudson sent word of his findings to the merchants in Amsterdam and requested their approval of further investigation. By the time he received a response—a summons to come to Amsterdam immediately—King James I had got wind of his discovery of a marvelous river that led deep into the American continent. James forbade Hudson and the English members of his crew to leave England, implying that there was a whiff of treachery about their working for the Dutch. Certainly the Netherlanders were quick to exploit the area Hudson had opened up, establishing a fur trade with the Indians that would lead in 1626 to the purchase of Manhattan Island and to the founding of New Amsterdam.

The English now were determined to secure Hudson's services for themselves, and in 1610 a group of prominent men in London, with the encouragement of James I's son Henry, Prince of Wales, commissioned Hudson to try the one corner of the North Atlantic that still seemed to guard its secrets. The expedition left on April 17, 1610, in Waymouth's old ship, the *Discovery,* with 20 men and two boys, including Hudson's son John, who was now in his mid-teens and was sailing with his father for the fourth time. The crew was of curious composition, considering that Hudson could offer good wages and should have been able to take his pick of the best seamen. Perhaps the most curious member of the party was the quaintly named Abacuck Prickett, a former haberdasher who had traded the world of buckles and buttons for a post as a serving-man to Sir Dudley Digges, one of the main sponsors of Hudson's voyage. Prickett was along presumably to keep watch over the interests of the ship's owners. Virtually all that is known about the personalities and conflicts of this ill-fated voyage comes from the account he wrote upon his return to England.

Four of the crew had sailed with Hudson before. Michael Perse and Arnold Lodlo had been members of Hudson's second voyage to seek a passage to the northeast, as had the carpenter Philip Staffe, a man whose steadfast character would be sorely tried this time out. The other old hand was the irascible Robert Juet, who was making his third trip with Hudson. Hudson had again appointed Juet first mate, but this mark of the captain's confidence in him would neither improve the man's disposition nor secure his loyalty.

With two exceptions, most of Hudson's other choices for the expedi-

tion either were nondescript or were further evidence that this veteran explorer was a singularly poor judge of character. John King, the quartermaster, though a moody personality, was competent enough in his job; and the rather colorless Robert Bylot would, in the end, prove a surprisingly good navigator. But William Wilson, one of the mariners, had few—if any—redeeming qualities: Surly and quick to take offense, he was a born troublemaker.

The same and more might be said of a young man named Henry Greene, whom Hudson, according to Prickett, "would have to sea with him because he could write so well." Innuendo surrounds the relationship between Hudson and the florid, mercurial young rogue. "By his lewd life and conversation hee had lost the good will of all his friends, and had spent all that hee had," Prickett wrote. But Hudson had taken a liking to him, had given him "meate, and drinke, and lodging," and had managed to persuade Greene's mother that she should contribute four pounds toward outfitting her son for the sea. For reasons that were never explained, Greene boarded the ship not at St. Katherine's Pool by the Tower of London with the others, but 20 miles downstream at Gravesend, and was not registered in the owners' books—a circumstance Prickett took pains to note. Some accounts hint that both Greene and Hudson had homosexual leanings. Whether that is true or not, Greene was soon to betray his patron's trust.

The *Discovery* reached Iceland on May 11. Held up because of fog and contrary winds, the voyagers bathed in the island's hot springs, fished, shot wild fowl, and quarreled. Greene picked a fight with the surgeon, and Hudson took Greene's side, telling Prickett to keep out of it, for "the surgeon had a tongue that would wrong the best friend hee had." Later, Juet, drunk, asserted that Greene was Hudson's lower-deck spy. By the time Hudson learned this, the ship was already on course for the enticing coastal gap that had been described by Davis. Though he was tempted to turn back and dump Juet in Iceland, Hudson reconsidered, and the matter was dropped. On June 25 the ship entered the strait that is now known by Hudson's name.

Within a few days ice floes and strong currents—which at their emergence from the strait cause the turbulence Davis had noticed—forced Hudson and his company south into Ungava Bay, which opens out of the strait's southern shore. The ice continued to block their westward progress, hemming the ship in until, as Prickett wrote, "wee could goe no further. Here our master was in despaire, and (as he told me after) he thought he should never have got out of the ice, but there have perished." Three weeks passed before they were able to break free, and long before that the company had resumed quarreling. Surly Juet scoffed at Hudson's hope "of seeing Bantam by Candlemasse"—meaning Java by early February. Hudson's offer to turn back if a majority wanted it only heightened their differences. Francis Clemens, the boatswain, declared "that if he had an hundred pounds, hee would give foure-score and ten to be at home," Prickett wrote, "but the carpenter,"—sturdy Philip Staffe—"made answere, that if hee had a hundred, hee would not give ten upon such condition."

The argument was interrupted by the need to save the ship from being

This 25-inch globe, created at the end of the 16th Century by the Englishman Emery Molyneaux, was hailed as including "the newest, secretest and latest discoveries"—notably those of Frobisher and Davis. Because the globe, unlike plane charts, allowed for the convergence of the meridians of longitude, Arctic explorers found it an invaluable aid to navigation.

Persistent attempts to decipher two bays

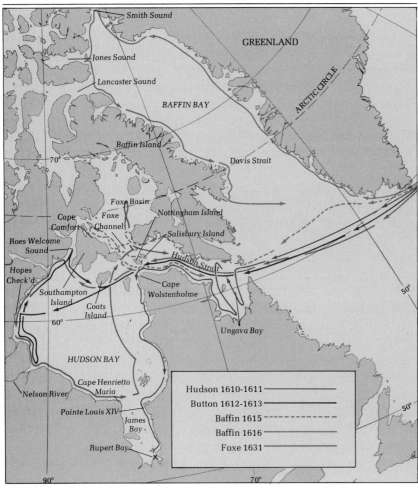

Smith Sound
Jones Sound
Lancaster Sound
GREENLAND
ARCTIC CIRCLE
BAFFIN BAY
Baffin Island
Davis Strait
70°
Foxe Basin
Cape Comfort
Foxe Channel
Nottingham Island
Salisbury Island
Roes Welcome Sound
Hudson Strait
Hopes Check'd
Cape Wolstenholme
Southampton Island
Coats Island
60°
Ungava Bay
50°
HUDSON BAY
Nelson River
Cape Henrietta Maria
Pointe Louis XIV
James Bay
Rupert Bay
50°

Hudson 1610-1611
Button 1612-1613
Baffin 1615
Baffin 1616
Foxe 1631

90°   70°

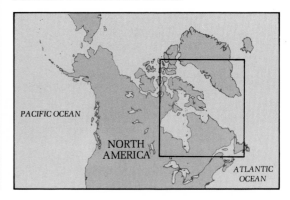

PACIFIC OCEAN
NORTH AMERICA
ATLANTIC OCEAN

Henry Hudson, Thomas Button and Luke Foxe all focused their search for the Northwest Passage on Hudson Bay; William Baffin, on his first voyage, probed Hudson Strait. Baffin then returned to explore both sides of the bay that would be named after him, but he lingered only briefly at Lancaster Sound, not realizing that it held a viable route to the west.

crushed by mountainous icebergs. This done, Hudson rendered the argument moot by continuing to sail west. At one point the men chased and lost a polar bear. "When she saw us looke at her," wrote Prickett, "she cast her head betweene her hinde legges, and then dived under the ice; and so from one piece to another, till she was out of our reach." It was sporting diversion, but the sullen crew was only briefly amused; they carried on their complaints in private.

In early August the little ship passed between a pair of 1,000-foot-high headlands that Hudson promptly named after two of his staunchest backers: To the south, swathed in clouds of crying sea fowl, rose the stepped cliff he called Cape Wolstenholme, while two miles away to the north, the sheer face of Cape Digges soared into the summer air. The captain sent Prickett, with Greene, Bylot and a few others, to reconnoiter Cape Digges (which the men soon found was actually an island rather than part of the northern mainland). They reported seeing deer, fresh sorrel and cliffs full of nesting birds. Prickett stumbled upon several cairns that turned out to be "full of fowles hanged by their neckes"—apparently a cache left by Eskimos.

The men urged Hudson to stay a few days on this island of plenty, but the captain would not hear of it. In front of him was spread a wide open sea, and he was "confidently proud," wrote a 17th Century chronicler named Samuel Purchas, "that he had won the passage." Hudson was sanguine that they would come upon more and better replenishment for their provisions farther on.

For a few weeks the ship plied a southerly course down the east side of the enormous bay—more accurately, an inland sea—that now bears Hudson's name. A clear run of some 400 miles, with nothing to the west but scattered islands, raised the captain's spirits higher. In the next 100 miles, the shore began to trail to the southwest, then to the west. This was a good sign: If he was, as he believed, sailing over the top of North America, Cathay would be somewhere to the west. But then, rounding what is now Pointe Louis XIV, he found that the shore veered to the south again. To his dismay, it continued in this direction for more than 200 miles and then began a slow curve back up to the north. Hudson had reached the bottom of what was later named James Bay, a short extension of Hudson Bay itself.

The sensible course would have been to follow the coastline, in hopes it would turn west again and bring him to the Pacific—or, at worst, show him that for the last 700 miles he had been exploring a cul de sac. But instead of breaking out of the trap of James Bay, Hudson sailed back and forth within it. "Up to the north we stood," wrote Prickett, "till we raised land, then downe to the south, and up to the north, then downe againe to the southe." The captain appeared to be sinking into a gulf of indecision. Perhaps he guessed that Hudson's Bay was what it was, a dead end, from which there could be no escape this year. Or he may have hoped to find some small outlet that would at least take him south to the vicinity of the upper Hudson River or the St. Lawrence. Possibly he was becoming deranged. No one will ever know.

Whatever the explanation for Hudson's strange actions, the chronic sore of mutiny began to fester once again. In early September, Juet's continuing complaints sparked an accusation of treachery from Hudson. The first mate insisted on being given an open trial—imprudently, since the resulting testimony from several members of the ship's company was enough to hang him. One said that Juet had threatened "to turne the head of the ship home from the action." Both Arnold Lodlo and Philip Staffe swore that he had advised them to keep close by their swords and muskets, which would be "charged with shot ere the voyage was over." Hudson was lenient, merely demoting Juet and raising Robert Bylot to first mate. But then he demoted Francis Clemens as well, making William Wilson the new boatswain. Juet now had company in his bitter disgruntlement.

As the season wore on, Hudson continued his wanderings in James Bay until, even if he had wanted to escape from it, he was finally blocked by ice. On November 1 the *Discovery* dropped anchor in what is now known as Rupert Bay, a shallow harbor that is sheltered by three hills, in the southeast corner of James Bay. By November 10 the vessel was solidly frozen in.

Hudson could hardly have found a more desolate spot in which to spend the winter. The low, muddy shore was backed by stunted Arctic willows, juniper and pine, eking out a meager life among lichen and moss. Hudson rued an earlier decision not to salt down some birds at Digges Island. The men calculated that, if they were very careful, it might be possible for them to stretch the ship's provisions until the spring thaw released the vessel; they could then go back "to the capes where the fowle bred," Prickett wrote, "for that was all the hope we had to bring us home."

The prospect of several months on short rations did little to restore the crew's faith in the captain's judgment. Nor were the men encouraged by Hudson's improvidence over the matter of a hut. Carpenter Philip Staffe had suggested that they build one right away, but Hudson inexplicably rejected the idea. Some two weeks later, he changed his mind and instructed Staffe to proceed. The carpenter for once refused. "The snowe and the frost were such as hee neither could nor would goe in hand with such worke," Prickett wrote. At that, Hudson "ferreted him out of his cabin to strike him, and calling him by many foule names, and threatening to hang him." It was no way to treat one of the men who were still loyal to him, but Hudson seems to have been incapable of dealing consistently with his crew.

A little earlier, the gunner, John Williams, had sickened and died. Following nautical custom, there was an auction of his belongings, from which the proceeds would be given to his family. Arbitrarily, Hudson removed a coat from the auction and sold it separately to Greene, who needed one. There were murmurs among the men, but if Hudson expected gratitude from his reprobate favorite, he was disappointed. In the aftermath of Hudson's quarrel with Staffe, Greene, whose malice had already sharpened several conflicts, made himself more than usually friendly to the carpenter, joining him on shooting expeditions on the shore. In a rage of jealousy, Hudson took the coat from Greene and gave it to Bylot. When Greene remonstrated, Hudson attacked his loose character, dishonesty and bad manners, and threatened to withhold his wages when the trip was over.

Discontent deepened as winter set in. Frostbite and scurvy were rife. The only bright note, Prickett wrote, was an abundance of the tiny willow ptarmigan—like "partridges white as milke"—of which they managed to kill "above an hundred dozen." But as spring approached, even the ptarmigan departed, and though flights of migrating geese and ducks passed over, they were not so easily caught. Soon the men were scavenging for anything at all edible, "how vile soever," Prickett wrote. "The mosse of the ground, than the which I take the powder of a post to bee much better, and the frogge (in his ingendering time as loathsome as a toade) was not spared."

In the midst of this famine, a lone Indian appeared at the ship. Hudson gave him a looking glass, a knife and some buttons, and the man came back the next day with several skins. The sailors' spirits rose at the prospect that he might be induced to bring food. But after this visit the man was never seen again.

Now, however, the ice began to break up sufficiently so that the ship's boat could be moved about. The men tried their hand at fishing. The first day's haul was enormous: "Five hundred fish, as big as good herrings, and some troutes," Prickett reported, "put us all in some hope to have our wants supplied." Assuming that the sea would continue to provide, the men consumed their catch, without salting down any of it. Unfortunately, subsequent catches were scarcely enough to warrant the effort the men expended. Then Hudson took the ship's boat and went off for a week, Prickett wrote, "to see if he could meet with the people" whose presence he had deduced from wisps of smoke to the south. He hoped to get meat, but the wary Indians eluded him, and he returned to the *Discovery* empty-handed.

It was now June. After seven long, miserable months, the *Discovery* was at last no longer icebound. But as the preparations for departure were started, Hudson compounded his offenses of the previous autumn. He removed Bylot from his position as first mate—the reason for his action is unclear—and put Philip Staffe, with whom he had mended his earlier quarrel, in his place. Then, Prickett wrote, Hudson confiscated all the navigation instruments on board. The two actions shocked and outraged the crew. For all his craftsmanly skill, Staffe could neither read nor write; and with everyone else precluded from reckoning the ship's course, Prickett wrote, the men believed that "the master and his ignorant mate would carry the ship whither the master pleased." Many feared that it was Hudson's intention to take them even deeper into the perilous unknown.

Just before the *Discovery* sailed, Hudson divided up the last of the bread and shared it out—about a pound for each man. It was an extraordinary thing to do. Predictably, many of the men bolted down in a day or two what was intended to last them for a fortnight. A few days later, after they were under way and the bread was virtually gone, Hudson divided the remaining cheese, about three and a half pounds a man, and issued that as well. Several of the crew suspected that Hudson had hidden stores of food for himself and his favorites, and their resentment was inflamed when Hudson, similarly suspicious, ordered a search of the men's lockers for secret caches.

According to testimony given later by the ship's surgeon, the spark that finally touched off mutiny was an indiscreet remark made by the carpenter. When Staffe was asked by boatswain William Wilson "why the master should soe favour to give meate to some of the companie, and not the rest," Staffe answered that "it was necessary that some of them should be kepte upp." Wilson reported this remark to Henry Greene, and the implication that there were some members of the crew whose welfare did not matter to Hudson was all the excuse Greene needed to arouse the crew to rebellion.

On the night of June 23, Greene and Wilson appeared in Prickett's cabin to announce their plan. They were going to commit Hudson, his son and the weakest of the crew to the shallop, and leave them to fend for themselves. Since most of them were illiterate, they needed Prickett to do some sympathetic editing of Hudson's log and later to plead their case with his former master, Sir Dudley Digges. (Prickett's account of the mutiny has always been treated warily for this reason.) If he refused, he could join Hudson in the shallop.

Prickett, now lamed by scurvy, was horrified. "I told them I marvelled to heare so much from them, considering that they were married men, and had wives and children," he wrote, "and that for their sakes they should not commit so foule a thing in the sight of God." Greene replied that "he would rather be hanged at home then starved abroad." A determined nucleus of the ship's crew—seven men in all, including old Robert Juet—were agreed. Weighing his own chances of survival, Prickett gave way under protest.

At dawn the plan went into action. While some of the men engaged Staffe in conversation to distract him from what was taking place, Hudson, emerging from his cabin, was bound with a rope and bundled into the shallop. John King and Thomas Woodhouse—both of them considered loyal to the captain—received similar treatment. Four more seamen, all subdued by sickness, were forced down into the little boat. Young John Hudson followed.

The mutineers might have called a halt there, but the shallop was to hold still one more person: the redoubtable Philip Staffe. His skills would have been useful on the *Discovery*, and the mutineers wanted him to remain. But the carpenter's unfailing loyalty prevailed. Nothing but force would keep him on board, he said. He damned the mutineers and their offer to spare him. Trust in God and love of his master were better, wrote the chronicler Samuel Purchas, "than with such villaines to accept of likelier hopes." Asking for his clothes and his tools, Staffe willingly went to his doom.

The shallop was cut loose. "Then out with their topsayles," Prickett wrote, "and towards the east they stood in a cleere sea," leaving nine men to fend for themselves with only one small sack of meal for sustenance. As soon as the shallop was out of sight, the mutineers hove to and ransacked the ship. In the hold, according to Prickett, they found some meal, two small casks of butter, some pork and half a bushel of peas. "But in the masters cabin we found 200 of bisket cakes, a pecke of meale, of beere to the quantitie of a butt." Suddenly someone cried that the shallop was drawing near. Feverishly the mutineers hoisted sail and flew "as from an enemy," Prickett wrote. Eventually the little boat and its condemned cargo receded into the bleak distance. Nothing was ever seen of them again.

For Captain Greene, as he now allowed himself to be called, triumph was short-lived. The conspirators hoped to sail the *Discovery* back to England and make their case as best they were able. But without Hudson there were doubts as to whether anyone was capable of finding the way. Juet and Bylot argued vehemently about the course to be taken. Juet thought they should head northwest, but Bylot firmly and correctly insisted on a northeasterly course—and succeeded in bringing the *Discovery*, at the end of July, back to Digges Island. Relief rose to elation as, on shore, they encountered some Eskimos who seemed, Prickett noted, "the most simple and kind people of the world." The next day Greene took Prickett, Wilson and three others in the ship's boat to meet and barter with the Eskimos, who had promised to bring venison. "When we came neere the shoare," wrote Prickett, "the people were on the hils dancing and leaping."

Prickett, who was still lame, remained on guard in the ship's boat while the others—of whom only Greene was armed, and he only with a broken pike—clambered ashore. The Eskimos appeared to be interested in bartering, but they had brought no meat, and Greene "swore they should have nothing till he had venison," wrote Prickett. Two of the Englishmen moved off to pick some sorrel. Suddenly the Eskimos attacked on two fronts. One had swum out to the boat, hauled himself over the side, produced a knife, and attacked the astonished Prickett. Slashed on his chest, thigh, right arm and left hand, the convalescent haberdasher nevertheless managed to summon strength enough to retaliate. He grabbed his own knife, and shortly found himself plunging it into the other's throat.

On land, four of the five Englishmen were attacked at the same moment and stabbed in the stomach. One died on the spot; the others staggered back toward the boat. The man who had escaped injury leaped into the water and swam for his life. Michael Perse, one of the wounded men, grabbed a hatchet from the boat and felled an Eskimo who was pursuing him. Greene swung and jabbed his absurdly inadequate weapon and cried encouragement to his fellows. Frantically they pushed off, but just as it seemed that they had escaped, the Eskimos released a salvo of arrows. Prickett and Perse were wounded. Greene fell dead. Andrew Motter, the man who had swum out from shore, now was hauled into the boat and helped row it back to the ship, which lay out of sight of the battle. Before they climbed aboard, the survivors unceremoniously threw Henry Greene's body into the sea, his brief career as captain ended. William Wilson died of his wounds later that day—"swearing and cursing in most fearefull manner," Prickett wrote—and Michael Perse two days afterward.

Now they were down to nine men. The journey ahead of them was long and perilous, and their larder dangerously depleted. Crossing over to Cape Wolstenholme, they managed to kill 200 sea fowl. When contrary winds kept them there, they killed 100 more. Then the wind turned favorable, and the *Discovery* at last could shape a course for home. The passage of Hudson Strait, assisted by the same current that had frustrated them on the outward journey, was accomplished in under two weeks instead of nearly five. But there remained more than 2,000 miles of the Atlantic to cross, and their ordeal was far from over. Head winds slowed their passage, and their weakened handling of the ship slowed it even more. Once again they were threatened by starvation. When the last of the sea fowl had been consumed, the men ate the bones fried in candle grease—with vinegar added for flavor. The concoction "made a good dish," Prickett recorded.

Toward the end, the old agitator Juet "dyed for meere want," Prickett reported, "and all our men were in despair." They were convinced that they had overshot Ireland, for which they were aiming, and had ceased to care "which end went forward." Robert Bylot, with an admirable display of stamina, worked the *Discovery* virtually singlehandedly and finally brought it home.

The remnants of the crew of the *Discovery* reached England in September 1611 and were questioned by maritime authorities the following

Resplendent in court attire, Sir Thomas Button rests one hand on a globe, casually indicating the Arctic shores he helped to discover. Although his voyage of 1612 suggested that Hudson Bay was a cul de sac, the Welsh captain fully expected the quest for the Northwest Passage to end successfully. "I doe confidently beleave there to be a passadge," he said, "as I doe there is one between Calais and Dover."

month. The emaciated condition of those who had returned, the deaths of those primarily responsible for the mutiny, the remote possibility that Hudson might still be alive, and the generally accepted belief that the *Discovery's* voyage had unfolded a vital segment of the Northwest Passage were all factors in the subsequent delay and indecision over bringing the mutineers to justice. Bylot in particular, with the qualities he had evinced in bringing the ship home and with the experience he had acquired, was more valuable on a ship's quarter-deck than stretching a rope on the gallows.

There were inquiries, tribunals, reprimands and popular slurs, but there was no trial for mutiny. Finally, in 1618, seven years after their return, four men—including Prickett but not Bylot—were arraigned. The charge was murder of Hudson and the rest. No convincing proof was offered—the four blamed Greene and Wilson as instigators—and they were acquitted.

Despite the horrors of the expedition, the very real exploratory achievements stirred such excitement that preparations for another voyage began almost immediately. Hudson had charted the east side of the bay, but what lay to the west remained entirely unknown. Moreover, Bylot had reported a tremendous flood tide from the west—a circumstance that was widely regarded as evidence of an opening to the Pacific. Thus it was that, in the spring of 1612, some 160 merchant-adventurers and the ever-enthusiastic Henry, Prince of Wales, dispatched Thomas Button to follow up on Hudson's discoveries. A Welshman who had seen naval service in Ireland and the West Indies, Button commanded an expedition consisting of his flagship, the *Resolution*, and Hudson's old *Discovery*. Two members of the company who must have had mixed feelings about their destination were Abacuck Prickett and Robert Bylot, who went along as guides.

Concerned that mutinous history not repeat itself on this voyage, Prince Henry gave Button explicit instructions for the government of both his ships and men. Daily prayers were required, and Sundays were to be "christianlike observed with godlie meditation." Quarreling, profanity, blasphemy, drunkenness and lewd behavior were to be punished without fail, and the captain was bound "to prevent all Mutynie amongst your people, and to preserve them as muche as maie be from the Treacherie and villanie of the Salvages and other Easterne people." Whether owing to these instructions, to the better temper of the crew, or to Button's own qualities as a leader, the expedition would suffer none of the internal strife that had plagued Hudson.

Button's sailing orders were equally precise: He was to sail along the northern side of Hudson Strait, then continue west, carefully observing the action of the tide. "If it come in Southwest, then you maie be sure the passage is that waie; if from the North or Northwest, your course must be to stand upp into it." Although some contemporary accounts say that Button was supposed to search for Hudson, his instructions from Prince Henry make no mention of such an assignment, and in fact he did not attempt to do so.

The expedition reached Digges Island without incident, but there trouble struck. Button commandeered canoes from some unwilling Eski-mos—the same Eskimos, perhaps, who had attacked Greene and his conspirators the year before—and five of his men were killed in the fracas that ensued. Button then moved on into the bay, steered south-westward past what is now Coats Island, with the promise of clear sail-ing ahead. Then, on August 13, he came on the barren tundra of the bay's western shore. With no apparent passage through to the Pacific, he named his landfall Hopes Check'd.

Now a storm blew up, and Button headed south to look for shelter. Two days later he entered a river, which he named the Nelson after a member of the company who died there. Wild fowl were plentiful, and it appeared to be a decent spot in which to spend the fast-approaching winter. Button ordered that a barricade be built to protect the ships from snow, ice and wind, and the crew settled in. During the long, dark months that followed, several men died; but Button kept the company's morale up, partly by encouraging discussions (in the form of written questions and answers) of the course they should pursue in the spring. When the ice finally permitted the ships to depart in June, he had a willing crew behind him.

Probably following the recommendation of Josiah Hubart, the pilot of the *Resolution*, Button headed north upon emerging from the Nelson. Hubart apparently had noted a flood tide that came from the east, and had conceived the notion that it originated from around some headland to the north of Hopes Check'd—"which headlands being founde," he wrote, "I do assure myselfe that the tyde will be found to come from the Westward." Button coasted northward until increasingly shallow water and a vague suggestion of land to the north (bad weather at this time considerably reduced visibility) led him to conclude that he was in a bay. In fact, he had entered a sound, later named Roes Welcome. Hav-ing charted 600 miles of coastline altogether, Button turned around and retraced his route to England, where he arrived in September 1613, after an absence of 16 months.

Button had carried out his assigned task with the utmost efficiency, and his findings seemed to indicate that the vast stretch of water Hudson had discovered was in fact a dead end. But he had not proved it. The southwest coast of Hudson Bay had still to be explored, and Roes Welcome was still, strictly speaking, an unknown quantity. Ultimately this did not matter, for the sound was not part of any passage to the Pa-cific. Nevertheless, a narrowing down of the options was becoming in-creasingly important.

Button himself, though disappointed not to have found it, believed the passage existed, for on his homeward journey he had paused—as in-structed—to study the tides between Digges and Nottingham Islands. Off the west side of Nottingham Island, he had discerned a strong flood from the north-northwest, which "must direct whomsoever shall seeke the passage hereafter."

He was not alone in his optimism. A group of nearly 300 adventurers with a lengthy and hopeful name—the Company of Merchants of Lon-don, Discoverers of the Northwest Passage—had been granted a royal charter for exploration to the west of Hudson Strait, in July of the pre-

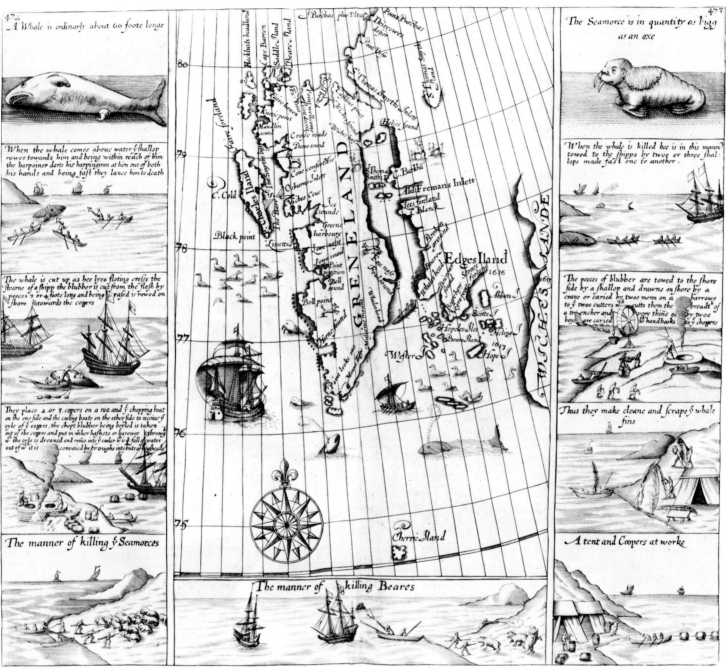

In decorative vignettes bordering a 17th Century map of Spitsbergen (then called Greneland), sailors harpoon whales, strip them of their blubber and render the fat into oil. Many an Arctic explorer—most notably William Baffin—learned to maneuver ships in ice-filled waters by serving in a Spitsbergen whaling fleet.

vious year, three months after Button had embarked on his own voyage. Many of his old backers were part of this new Northwest Passage Company, as it came to be called, and they were eager to follow up on his findings. In March 1614, William Gibbons, who had sailed with Button, set forth in the *Discovery* to continue the search. Button had highly recommended the man, who happened to be a relative. But Gibbons either was wildly incompetent or had terrible luck. He spent 10 weeks trapped by ice in an inlet on the coast of Labrador; and when he finally managed to get out, the season was so far gone that he had to return home, having accomplished absolutely nothing.

Undaunted, the company put together another attempt. The following spring the good ship *Discovery* was sent forth once again. Her captain was Robert Bylot, her pilot a gifted mariner named William Baffin. Very little is known of Baffin's origins, but he may have been a native of London or Westminster. He learned his navigational skills in the Muscovy Company's prospering Spitsbergen whaling fleet, and he was famil-

Two pages from William Baffin's logbook for a voyage to the Arctic in 1615 bear witness to his remarkable gifts as a navigator. His estimations of longitude, based on observations of the moon and involving laborious computations, were often accurate to within 1°.

iar with a method of determining longitude by observing the moon's culmination, or highest altitude. Apart from the laborious calculations involved in the method, Baffin was hampered in this technique by the crudity of the instruments that were at his disposal. But he was the first to attempt to make a lunar observation at sea, and was certainly among the best scientific navigators of his day. His charting, surveys, soundings and records of tides and currents were scrupulous, and would win praise 200 years later from navigators with access to far more accurate equipment.

The present trip was remarkable for the deductions his close observations enabled him to make. After "an indifferent good passage," he wrote in his journal, the voyagers reached Resolution Island at the end of May. Progress through Hudson Strait was slowed by contrary winds and thick ice, and July was upon them before they reached the southwestern corner of the huge island later named in Baffin's honor. Here the grinding of enormous ice floes put the ship in considerable danger. "For sometymes the ship was hoysed aloft," Baffin wrote, "and at other tymes shee havinge, as it were, got the upper hand, would force great mighty peeces of ice to sinke down on the one side of hir, and rise on the other." After several hours of this, the explorers managed to stand away to the north—roughly in the direction Button had indicated—where they found the sea relatively clear of ice. But the farther north they went (in what is now Foxe Channel), the shoaler was the water and the more ice they encountered. After circling east and having no better luck, they made for the west.

On July 12 they were off the northeast side of what is now Southampton Island. Here the flood seemed to come from the north, Baffin wrote, which "put us in great hope of a passage this way." Bylot named a nearby headland Cape Comfort in anticipation. But when they rounded the cape they found more ice, increasingly shallow water and "smale showe of any tyde," Baffin reported. Clearly the long-sought channel did not lie here. After spending 17 days observing the play of tides in the western mouth of Hudson Strait, the *Discovery* made for home, anchoring at Plymouth on September 8.

Baffin's verdict was that any "floods" that were perceived as coming from the west were probably caused by Atlantic tides, and that there was no passage to a western sea to be discovered through Hudson's Strait. Instead, he urged that the investigation now be directed to the far north, up the broad strait between Greenland and Baffin Island that Davis had opened to view. Baffin's decisions were readily accepted by his sponsors. Moreover, they remained entirely confident of the success of the expedition, as indicated in their instructions for a second voyage: "If you can so compasse it without danger," Baffin was told, regarding his predicted arrival in Japan, "we would have you to bring home one of the men of the countrey."

Embarked once more in the old *Discovery* in March 1616, Baffin and Bylot rounded the southern tip of Greenland in mid-May and began a steady progress up along its western coast, passing Sanderson's Hope— the northernmost point reached by Davis—at the end of the month. Thereafter, head winds and ice hampered them so much that on June 10 they made a decision to head for Greenland's shore, "till such time as the ice were more wasted and gone," Baffin wrote, "for we plainely saw that it consumed very fast." Eight days later, when they headed north once again, the sea was virtually clear. The weather, on the other hand, was uncooperative. Almost every day brought snow, Baffin reported, and "on Midsummer day, our shrowds, roapes and sailes were so frozen that we could scarce handle them; yet the cold is not so extreame, but it may well be endured."

In early July they entered Smith Sound, named by Baffin after one of his backers. They were now just north of 78°, the highest latitude reached by Baffin. Three days of efforts to go ashore for a reconnaissance were balked by foul weather. Finally, with a stiff wind at their backs, the voyagers gave up and stood to the west. Early on July 10, "at which time it fell calme and very foggie," Baffin wrote, they found themselves at the entrance of another inlet, which they named Alderman Jones Sound after another sponsor. "Having an easie gale of wind east north-east, we ranne along by the shore," reported Baffin, adding laconically that the shore "now trendeth much south, and beginneth to shew like a bay." Unless something opened up to the west, it looked as though Baffin Bay—as this sea north of Davis Strait was later named—would prove yet another dead end.

The western shore of Baffin Bay is deeply indented with fjords, and behind them are snow-covered mountains that rise to heights of 8,000 feet. Light plays curious tricks in the ice and snow fields of the Arctic, and it is never easy to estimate the potential of a given opening. On July 12, Baffin passed a broad sound, some 40 miles across, which he named Lancaster Sound, in honor of yet another sponsor. He apparently decided from the aspect of the background mountains and the disposition of ice on the sea that the opening would lead nowhere. Two centuries would pass before another explorer proved him in error. "Here our hope of passage began to be lesse every day," Baffin wrote, "for from this Sound to the southward wee had a ledge of ice betweene the shoare and us, but cleare to the seaward."

For nearly 900 miles the ice that hugged the eastern coast of Baffin Island kept the *Discovery* far from the shore, and convinced her pilot that there was no sea route between the mountains. In late July the voyagers were back in territory that had already been checked by Davis 30 years before. "And seeing that wee had made an end of our discovery, and the yeare being too farre spent to goe for the bottome of the bay to search for drest finnes"—meaning whalebone—"therefore wee determined to goe for the coast of Groineland to see if we could get some refreshing for our men."

One member of the company had already died of scurvy. Three more were seriously sick. It was established that fresh greens were a remedy for the disease, and on an island off Greenland, Baffin reported, "we found great abundance of the herbs called scurvie grasse, which we boiled in beere, and so dranke thereof, using it also in sallets, with sorrell and orpen, which here groweth in abundance." The greens performed their healing work quickly: "All our men within eight or nine dayes space were in perfect health," Baffin noted, "and so continued till our arrival in England." Concerning the main purpose of the expedition, Baffin wrote to Sir John Wolstenholme, his chief patron, "There is no passage nor hope of passage, in the north of Davis Straights. We having coasted all, or neere all the circumference thereof, and finde it to be no other than a great bay."

Baffin's verdicts on his voyages to Hudson Strait and Baffin Bay had not simply narrowed the available options. The process of elimination appeared complete, and many accepted the opinion that there was no Northwest Passage after all. For more than a decade the English had made almost annual attempts to find the channel to Cathay. Baffin's failure effectively damped the ardor of the men whose money had financed these expeditions.

But not everyone gave up hope. The Danes now took up the quest. In 1619 they sent a two-ship expedition under Jens Munk to follow up the English discoveries to the north of North America. Munk spent a ghastly winter in Hudson Bay. At the end of nearly nine months, only he and two of his men were left alive—but they somehow managed to get back to Denmark, arriving in September 1620. This disaster was apparently sufficient to satisfy the Danes that there was no profit to be had in sending additional expeditions to seek a passage through such an inhospitable portion of the globe.

The English, on the other hand, seemed unable to resist the lure of the Arctic for long. Owing largely to the efforts of an old sea dog named Luke Foxe, British interest in finding the Northwest Passage was rekindled in 1631. By his own account, this exploration was one Foxe "had beene itching after" for some 25 years. Finally, at the age of 45, he secured the patronage of such influential Londoners as Sir Thomas Roe and that perennial supporter of Arctic voyaging, Sir John Wolstenholme. Not to be outdone, the merchants of Bristol equipped an expedition of their own, headed by Captain Thomas James. Both Foxe and James carried identical sailing instructions as well as letters of introduction from King Charles I to the Emperor of Japan.

The two captains presented an interesting contrast. Foxe was a practical mariner who had learned his craft from the pains and privations of long experience. He was not well educated, and tended to deride "mathematicall sea-men" who, when they put to sea, as he later wrote, "looke forthe and tremble at the rising of every wave." James, on the other hand, was a cultivated man but evidently had less boat-handling savvy than his rival, though he may have known more about scientific navigation. They also differed in their attitudes toward picking a crew: Foxe was eager to employ men who had previous experience in the Arctic, but found none; James refused several such men who applied to him, apparently dead set against having subordinates who might know more than he about what to expect.

In nautical terms, the expeditions were equally endowed. Foxe sailed the 70- or 80-ton pinnace *Charles*, with a crew of 20 men and two boys. James sailed the *Henrietta Maria*, of similar size and with the same number of crewmen. Both were provisioned for 18 months, and both departed in early May, within days of each other.

As things turned out, Foxe had slightly the better time of it. He entered Hudson Strait on June 22, and sighted Salisbury Island at its western end two and a half weeks later. Prevented by ice from continuing any farther north, Foxe rounded the south side of Coats Island and sailed across the mouth of Roes Welcome. When he reached the western shore of Hudson Bay, he followed it southward to the mouth of the Nelson River, where he halted for nearly two weeks in order to overhaul the ship. He then pressed on along the coast, and on August 29, about halfway between the Nelson River and the opening into James Bay, he encountered his rival. James entertained Foxe at a partridge dinner on board the *Henrietta Maria.* After the meal, Foxe confided to his diary: "I did perceive him to bee a practitioner in the mathematicks," adding, "I found that hee was no seaman." Foxe noted maliciously that a sudden squall "threw in so much water as wee could not have wanted sause if wee had had roast Mutton."

Soon Foxe was off again. On September 2 he reached Cape Henrietta Maria (so named shortly afterward by James), where the coast turns south into James Bay. Having thus charted the segment of Hudson Bay

A woodcut from Danish explorer Jens Munk's account of his 1619 voyage conflates two occasions when the crew disembarked on the south coast of Baffin Island. At one anchorage, the sailors were welcomed by Eskimos; at another landing place, miles from the first, the men shot a reindeer, and Munk named a nearby channel Reindeer Sound.

left unexplored by Button, Foxe veered north, across the middle of the bay, and less than a week later sighted Coats Island again. He then penetrated the channel that bears his name, and charted its eastern shore, reaching a latitude of 66°47′N. With his crew growing increasingly ill, Foxe abandoned further exploration and headed home. He was back in England at the end of October, having traversed more sea in six months than any of his predecessors.

James fared quite differently. Having sailed slowly into James Bay, where Hudson's tragedy had taken place 20 years before, his vessel struck a rock (not for the first time), and he was forced to jettison most of the coal that had been brought along as fuel for the ship's stoves. He then crisscrossed the bay for several weeks, until finally the thickening ice obliged him to stop for the winter. He had the men unload the ship and build three huts on shore.

James then took the extraordinary step of sinking his ship to save it from being pounded to pieces in the surf. Plugs were cut from the planking, and the hold was weighted with anchors, cables and tools. On November 29, as a storm drove the *Henrietta Maria* violently against the sand, the crew removed the plugs and let the water flow in. Several hours passed before the ship began to settle. As night drew on, James and his men contemplated what they had done. "Our men that were ashoare stood looking upon us," James wrote later, "almost dead with cold and sorrowes, to see our misery and their owne."

They spent the winter constructing a pinnace in the event that the ship could not be salvaged in the spring. Few of them believed it could. Most of the crewmen came down with scurvy, including the carpenter. In May he and another man died, bringing the total of their losses to four (two had died earlier in accidents). With the pinnace only half built, they decided to try to raise the *Henrietta Maria*. Many of them were scarcely able to walk, but with two iron bars and four broken shovels, they labored at breaking the ice and hauling it out of the ship. Incredibly, the task was accomplished. June was spent repairing the damage, and in early July, James set sail.

Emerging from James Bay, he was forced by ice to double back along the west coast of Hudson Bay. He then followed the route Foxe had taken through Foxe Channel, and explored the west of it until ice prevented further progress. At that point he headed for England, reaching it a year after Foxe's return.

Although both captains had failed in the quest, Foxe had done a superior job of charting what he had found, and he had not lost any men. Ironically, he was ridiculed for coming back so soon, while James, though he had accomplished not a whit more than Foxe, received a hero's welcome for the hardships endured in his wintering over—hardships that he described in graphic detail in a promptly published account of the voyage. In any event, both Foxe and James had strengthened Button's inference that there was no westerly outlet from Hudson Bay. They had also shown that whatever break there might be in the coastline of Foxe Basin, ice could be expected to make it impassable. Between them, they had sealed all hopes of finding a passage for several generations to come.

Chapter 3

Ambitious assaults on every front

Three supply ships of the Hudson's Bay Company, a fur-trading monolith that helped map the Canadian Arctic, leave England for wilderness outposts.

hen the search for the Northwest Passage came to a near halt in 1632, it was not simply because of doubts about the route's existence—although the long chain of failures in the quest, from Cabot and Gilbert to Foxe and James, had certainly made monarchs and merchants less willing to risk their money on such a dubious enterprise. Quite as important was the impulse to capitalize on the riches revealed by the explorers of America's northern coasts.

Fish, whales and timber were present along those coasts in what seemed like infinite abundance, and the hinterland of North America was teeming with another living and highly marketable treasure: its indigenous, sleek-furred mammals. Otter, ermine, marten, muskrat and mink were all hunted for their pelts, but the animal that was most avidly sought was the beaver—a three-foot-long genius of a rodent that could fell trees, dam lakes and build lasting lodges of sticks and mud, but was seldom able to escape the Indian who waited to trap it near its lakeside home. The beaver's smooth, dense fur, designed by nature to protect the semiaquatic animal from the bitter cold, had a fatal appeal to the Europeans' vanity and their love of fashion. Before long, no member of genteel society would be seen in public without a stylish, high-crowned beaver hat; men even bequeathed their favorite hats to deserving friends in their wills.

A redirecting of national energies away from exploration and toward exploitation was only part of the reason for the neglect of the Northwest Passage after Foxe and James, however. Another factor—one that only time could reveal—was that explorers had gone as far as they could. In spite of the skills and valor of Davis, Hudson, Baffin and the rest, nautical and mechanical knowledge would have to move in many directions before real progress toward fulfillment of the quest became possible. It would be more than a hundred years before a pilot could correctly gauge his longitude, and even longer than that before captains would know the diet necessary to keep their men alive and well during one, two and sometimes more Arctic winters. Before the search could go farther than it had already gone, ships would have to be stronger, and the bare outline of North America would have to be filled in by travelers on land. Had Baffin, instead of stating that the passage did not exist, simply denied the possibility of its attainment by him and his contemporaries, he would have been right.

Although the remainder of the 17th Century and most of the 18th disclosed scarcely an inch of sea-lane to the Pacific, the period saw a great deal of activity that would be crucial to later attempts. Some of this activity went on in blithe disregard of the problem of the passage. Some was specifically directed at a solution. Regardless of intention, it had the collective effect of bringing a solution nearer. Then, at the end of the 18th Century, a great mariner, Captain James Cook, would join the hunt. Thanks to all the disparate activities of traders and trappers, explorers and statesmen, scholars and surgeons, and to his own unique abilities, Cook would usher in a new dawn of possibility.

In the wake of the probes by Foxe and James, commercial entrenchment in the wilderness that bordered Hudson Bay came slowly. Begin-

The Hudson's Bay Company coat of arms is emblazoned with animals: A fox seated on an ermine-lined cap tops a shield flanked by moose and quartered by beavers. The Latin motto—A human skin for an animal skin—suggests the willingness of company traders to risk their lives in pursuit of the best pelts.

ning in 1642, England was distracted by a civil war and a decade of republican rule under Oliver Cromwell; and it was not until well after the restoration of Charles II to the throne in 1660 that Englishmen again ventured across the Atlantic to the northern shores of the American continent. Then, to their dismay, they discovered that the evident and substantial resources of the region were being resolutely preempted by the French. From bases on the St. Lawrence, the French had for some years been pushing westward, sending their agents out to barter with the Indians for skins and establishing trading posts that would ensure regular deliveries. After reaching Lake Superior, they had then penetrated northward in the direction of Hudson Bay itself.

By an odd twist of history, it was two Frenchmen who prodded the English into establishing their own network of routes, forts and trading

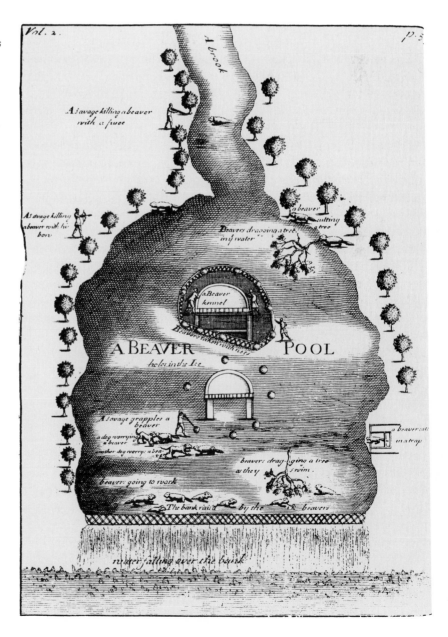

An instructional 18th Century engraving shows beavers at work gnawing down trees and raising a "bank," or dam. The sketch also reveals the Indians' ingenuity in hunting the animals—with traps, guns, bows and arrows, trained dogs and, in winter, by chipping holes in the ice and stretching out nets to ensnare beavers as they emerged from the water.

stations in the North American wilderness. Médard Chouart, Sieur des Groseilliers, and Pierre Esprit Radisson were partners by kinship and by calling. Brothers-in-law and fellow fur traders, the two men had been taxed heavily by their own government for daring to make an overland trip in search of furs—an escapade that was contrary to the official French policy of funneling furs along the St. Lawrence River. Indignant, they decided to go after English backing instead, and carried their proposals to the top. "Mr. Gooseberry" (as the English called Groseilliers) and Radisson paid a visit to King Charles II in 1665 and convinced him that Hudson Strait offered better access into the central wilderness than did the St. Lawrence—and that it would ultimately be more profitable. Impressed by what he was told, the King offered the two 40 shillings per week and supplied them with two ketches for the purpose of trading. They proved their point by gathering almost £1,500 worth of furs in a single voyage to Hudson Bay.

Three years later the English had built their first fort—Fort Charles, which was located at the southern end of James Bay—and had made a trading agreement with the local Cree Indians. Two years after this, in 1670, King Charles granted a charter to the newly formed "Governor and Company of Adventurers of England trading into Hudson's Bay," more commonly known as the Hudson's Bay Company. The terms of the charter were generous to the adventurers, if somewhat prodigal with what was, after all, Indian territory. It granted the company nothing less than the entire trade from one of the richest fur-producing regions in the world, including all fishing privileges and exclusive rights to "all Mynes Royall as well discovered as not discovered of Gold Silver Gemms and pretious Stones." The Hudson's Bay Company was also authorized to "make peace or Warre with any Prince or people whatsoever that are not Christians."

Within a few years the English had established five forts on the southern shore of Hudson Bay, and rates of exchange for beaver skins were standardized: a pound of tobacco for one skin, a laced coat for six, a fowling gun for 12. These terms were beneficial to everyone concerned, and thus trade prospered.

The English confined their own exertion to trading along the fractious waters of Hudson Strait during the three or four months of the year, from July to October, when travel was possible. There seemed no reason to become more deeply involved, since the company made huge profits, paying its investors annual dividends that ran as high as 50 per cent of the value of the stock.

Prosperity in the New World inevitably caused the English ardor for the Northwest Passage to abate somewhat. There were a few souls, however, who looked on the quest as more than a fanciful daydream. Among these was James Knight, an energetic but credulous septuagenarian who, during a working life spent with the Hudson's Bay Company, had often heard rumors of a passage from the company's Indian contacts—people with a habit of embroidering their tales in any way that might please their audience. Knight believed, because Indians had told him so, that 17 rivers lay north of Churchill, a trading post on the western shore of the bay; that one of them, the 15th, was almost awash with copper; that beyond it were limitless reserves of gold and silver; and that the 17th was the long-sought strait leading to the Pacific.

Knight's persistent and eloquent advocacy was more than the Hudson's Bay Company was able to resist; and in 1719, with the backing of the company's London committee, he fitted out two vessels, the 100-ton frigate *Albany* and the 40-ton sloop *Discovery*. In June, with high hopes and instructions "to preserve the Shipp, Sloop and Mens Lives," Knight and his company sailed out of Gravesend—and out of sight of their country forever. No member of either crew, 27 men in all, was ever found alive by a European. In 1722 a search party that had been sent north from Churchill picked up part of a ship's mast, a bit of cabin lining and a medicine chest, but failed to locate a relic that might solve the puzzle of the expedition's fate.

Half a century would elapse before any solid information about the disaster came to light. Then, in 1767, a whaling ship put in at Marble Island, some 300 miles north of Churchill. Men dispatched to collect driftwood discovered a small harbor on the southeast coast, accessible only at high tide. Within were two weather-beaten hulls and, nearby, some guns, anchors, cables, an anvil—and a skull.

Some aged local Eskimos were able to recall the final outcome of Knight's venture. Racked by hunger and disease, the Englishmen passed a catastrophic first winter on the island, and within a year only 20 were alive. Fifteen more were dead by the spring of 1721, in spite of the Eskimos' gifts of whale blubber and seal flesh, and summer saw three of the last five perish. According to the mate on the whaler, the Eskimos testified that the remaining "two survived many days after the rest, and frequently went to the top of an adjacent rock and earnestly looked to the south and east, as if in expectation of some vessels coming to their relief." Finally, "one of the two died, and the other's strength was so far exhausted that he fell down and died also in attempting to dig a grave for his companion."

There were enough relics to make positive identification of the ships, but no log or papers to elucidate the course of the tragedy. Whether the men died of scurvy or starvation, Knight's undertaking was a tragic failure—and one that might, but for chance, have been averted: Some English trading ships were off the coast of Marble Island in the summer of 1720, just two days' sailing time from the spot where Knight and his crews were languishing.

Despair over Knight's fate brought on a recurrence of the Hudson's Bay Company's old lethargy. This was unfortunate, because the cause of the Northwest Passage was about to be championed by a rare promotional genius, one Arthur Dobbs. A landowner and member of the Irish Parliament, Dobbs had already, by 1730, given his indefatigable attention to the questions of Irish trade and British colonial policy, and to the nature of the aurora borealis—the northern lights. He had also compiled a 70-page abstract of all journals that had been published by Arctic explorers since the search for a northwest passage began. His optimistic conclusion was that a passage indeed existed, and that its entrance —in spite of all the evidence to the contrary—lay in the northwestern corner of Hudson Bay.

Dobbs's reasoning was based mainly on the behavior of tides—which would have been an important clue had it been possible, in the first place, to gauge them accurately from the swaying deck of a ship and, in the second place, to compute their origins from such labyrinthine coastlines and undulating seabeds as those of Hudson Bay and Strait, and Foxe Channel and Basin. But Dobbs was a landsman at the mercy of scattered references spanning two centuries. He gleaned what he wanted from them, molding the facts to suit his enthusiasm. He also offered new evidence relating to the density of ice floes—a notoriously unreliable factor, since no one winter was identical with another—and leaned heavily on already discredited legends of past voyages and of Pacific islands where domestic pots and pans were made of gold and silver. Dobbs's arguments, in other words, had no more factual sophistication than those of Sir Humphrey Gilbert 150 years before.

In 1735 Dobbs found an effective ally in Christopher Middleton, one of the most distinguished of the Hudson's Bay Company captains. The company itself was less interested. Its main business of trade was flourishing, and it still saw little reason to dabble in foggy speculations. It had, as Dobbs accusingly pointed out, much to fear from the discovery of such a passage, since an easy route to the Pacific would "animate the rest of the merchants to pursue the trade," causing the company to "lose their beloved monopoly." Its governors therefore remained politely procrastinating. Nor was the government in any position to help. In 1740 England was fighting one war with Spain and it was sliding toward another with France.

Dobbs thus cried almost alone in the wilderness. But he cried loudly, and eventually was heard. His belief that a passage to the Pacific would give England a perfect means of attacking the Spanish—and "soon humble them, and make them value our Friendship"—reached the ears of George II. The King was impressed by the strategy, and no less by the likely expense of fitting out two ships—"such a Trifle, that it should not be obstructed on that Account." Obstruction forthwith ceased, and on June 8, 1741, the Admiralty sloop *Furnace*, carrying a crew of 34, and the 150-ton Admiralty coastal vessel *Discovery*, with 43 aboard, set sail. Thus commenced one of the shadier episodes in the history of the search for the Northwest Passage.

In command was Christopher Middleton of the Hudson's Bay Company. His main mission was to investigate the source of a powerful flood tide in Roes Welcome, the sound first seen by Button early in the 17th Century. The crews were even less disciplined than usual. They were not volunteers but, as was usual with Admiralty ships during wartime, the press-ganged flotsam of London slums. Not three of them were fit to man a ship, Middleton complained later; "no Ship was ever pester'd with such a Set of Rogues, most of them having deserv'd hanging before they enter'd with me."

Reaching Hudson Bay in late July after a delayed start from England, Middleton decided the season was too far advanced for serious exploration and put into Churchill for the winter. Although the Hudson's Bay Company had promised the help of its representatives who were stationed in the bay, inhabitants of Churchill were less than warm toward

This map—drawn by a clerk who sailed with Christopher Middleton, and dedicated to Arthur Dobbs—aimed at undermining Middleton's conclusion that no passage existed through Hudson Bay. Citing scouting trips made by an officer of the expedition (script, upper left), the clerk labeled Wager Inlet a "strait" and drew an imaginary outlet that, he said, "cannot be far from the Great Western Ocean."

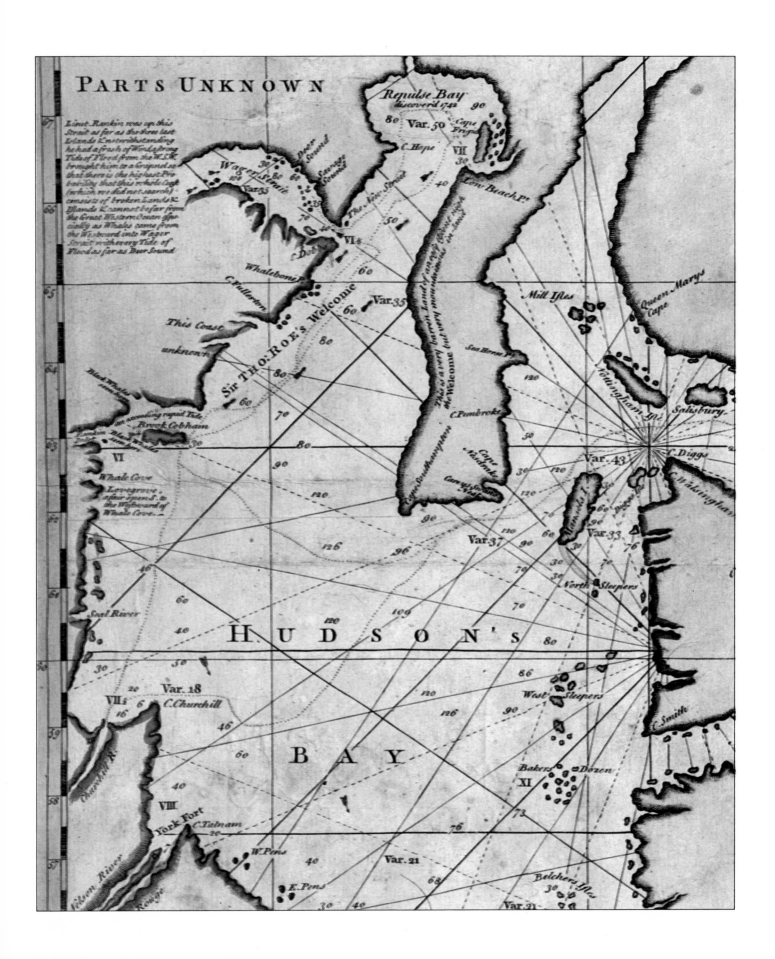

PARTS UNKNOWN

Repulse Bay
discover'd 1742

Var. 50

C. Hope

Lieut. Rankin was up this
Strait as far as the three last
Islands & notwithstanding
he had a fresh of Wind, a strong
Tide of Flood from the W.S.W.
brought him to a Serpent so
that there is the highest Probability that this whole Coast
(which we did not search)
consists of broken Lands &
Islands & cannot be far from
the Great Western Ocean especially as Whales came from
the Westward into Wager
Strait with every Tide of
Flood as far as Deer Sound

Wager Strait

Var. 35

C. Frigid

VII

Low Beach Pt

The New Strait

VI

Whalebone

C. Fullerton

Sir THO: ROE'S Welcome

This Coast

unknown

This is a very barren Land & except Close upon
the Welcome but very mountainous we had

Mill Isles

Queen Marys
Cape

Sea Horse Pt

Black Whales

Var. 35

Var. 35

Nottingham Ifle

Salisbury

Brook Cobham

C. Pembroke

C. Diggs

VI

Cape Southampton

Cape
Madoke

Carey Swans Nest

Var. 43

Whalebone

Whale Cove

Lovegrove
after opens to
the Westward of
Whale Cove

Mansels I.

Var. 33

Seal River

North Sleepers

H U D S O N'S

West Sleepers

C. Smith

Var. 18

VII

C. Churchill

B A Y

Churchill R.

Bakers Dozen

XI

VIII

York Fort

C. Talnam

W. Pens

Var. 21

Nelson River

Belchers Isles

E. Pens

Var. 21

Var. 21

newcomers—possibly justifiably, since Middleton had no qualms about luring good men away from the outpost "with Liquor, fine words and preferment" to enhance his own unreliable crews. Company employees also resented the prospect of having to share the region's meager resources of partridge, wild goose and caribou with the explorers—explorers, moreover, who proposed to do no exploring during the next nine months, and whose ultimate success, if it came, might present a serious threat to their own livelihood.

To make matters worse, Middleton's men suffered a nasty disappointment in the matter of shelter. They had expected to move into an abandoned fort that had been used a generation before by Knight. It was now, however, "nothing but a Heap of rubbish," requiring complete rebuilding. After it had been restored, the men shot what game they could, collected firewood and settled in for a winter that would be relieved only by generous allowances of brandy. As the ice thickened and smudges of scrub and sea turned winter-white under 10 feet of snow, they did what they could to keep warm.

It was impossible. Even with constantly stoked fires and red-hot balls of shot hanging in the windows, water quickly froze. Wine froze as it was poured into glasses, and stronger spirits congealed into the viscosity of olive oil. Scurvy, precipitated by the rampant consumption of alcohol, made its appearance and laid low a third of the combined company of about 80; by the end of the winter, 10 men had died of it. Those who emerged into the sunlight and thaw of May—many of them missing fingers and toes that had been amputated because of frostbite—were not the men they had been a year before.

Early in July 1742 the *Furnace* and the *Discovery* set sail for the north. Roughly 400 miles brought them to the approaches of Roes Welcome, which, despite Button's negative results in 1613, was still endowed by Dobbs with boundless possibilities. But as the crews penetrated the narrows, the ice grew deeper, until progress at times was possible only by the tedious methods of warping and towing. By mid-July they had passed lat. 65°N., where Middleton had orders to begin exploration. A few miles farther on, the expedition rounded a cape (which Middleton named Cape Dobbs after his restless supporter) and headed into a broad inlet. Middleton called this the Wager, in honor of the current First Lord of the Admiralty.

There was no strong eastward or southward flow of the currents to indicate that this might be the passage to the Pacific. None of the officers thought it was. Nevertheless, Middleton was not about to skimp his work: He conscientiously dispatched four separate parties to survey the inlet in small boats. Each returned with a negative report. Intriguingly, some black whales were seen within the sound, whereas none had been sighted at its opening. But the flood tide patently came from the east, and all the coves were icebound; the water at the farthest accessible point was found to be almost free of salt. It was therefore without misgivings that Middleton gave orders for the expedition to abandon Wager Inlet and stand to the north.

The next day a cape was spotted on the western shore. Nobody up to this time had suspected that Roes Welcome extended nearly so far to the

A two-ship expedition led by William Moor seeks anchorage for the winter of 1746-1747 in a small creek emptying into Hudson Bay. The winter was a cruelly cold one, locking the vessels in ice eight feet thick, and the following summer's search for westward egress from the bay yielded nothing but disappointment.

north; yet here was a prominent headland, and land stretching away from it to the west, which, wrote Middleton, "gives us great Joy and hopes of it's being the extream Part of America, on which Account I named it C. Hope." It took no more than a night of sailing to crush those high spirits. The land veered around to the north, then east, then south. In other words, they had come to yet another dead end, from which the only way out—apart from the way they had entered—was a strait, now thickly iced over, leading to the southeast: Frozen Strait, joining Roes Welcome with the waters of Foxe Basin. As if to underscore his frustration, Middleton baptized the obstinate curl of this shoreline Repulse Bay. Then, after some sketchy surveying of the coastline to the south, he returned to England.

Arthur Dobbs was far from pleased. He had no mind to be shown wrong by any man—even if that man had probed every mile of the coast in question while Dobbs himself had merely concocted geography in his library. He pored over Middleton's account of the journey, searching for flaws in the argument, and at last decided that he had found one. Wager Inlet, he declared, was the passage after all. With bookish, spurious arguments, he turned a noisy waterfall and other trivial details noted by Middleton into portents of a passage.

Then Dobbs trumped up something more sinister than false geography. Middleton, he claimed before the Board of the Admiralty, had deliberately covered up the existence of a passage. He was in cahoots with the Hudson's Bay Company, which had bribed him to keep his knowledge to himself. Dobbs even produced officers from the expedition to back up his claims. (The likelihood that he paid them well for doing so has never been proved, but it remains the most plausible explanation.) Dobbs had no personal dislike of Middleton, but sacrificing the explorer's reputation and career could be justified, in Dobbs's view, to advance his own campaign against the sloth and cupidity of the Hudson's Bay Company.

It was true that Middleton had been less than punctilious in the very last stage of his expedition, coasting a little too rapidly southward after the setback of Repulse Bay. Perhaps for this reason as much as any other, the Board of the Admiralty was not satisfied with his patient refutations when he was called before them in 1742 to answer Dobbs's charges. He was never again given an important command.

For the time being, Dobbs was having his way. At his instigation, Parliament in 1745 offered a £20,000 reward to any British subject who discovered a passage running westward from Hudson Bay (the size of the sum was certain to counter any offers the company might make to persuade explorers to suppress their discoveries). Those who disagreed with Dobbs—like Middleton, or a company captain named William Coats, who found Dobbs's topography "erronious" and "contrary to the experience and concurrent testimony of every person who have resided in that country"—were ignored.

Within a year of the announcement of the prize, an expedition of two ships was in preparation, organized by Dobbs himself and sponsored by some of the mightiest in the land, including peers, merchants and members of Parliament. Placed in command was William Moor. He was Christopher Middleton's cousin, had served as master on the *Discovery* four years before, and had written in his own account of the journey that "there is no Passage into the other Ocean between Churchill and the Latit. 67°N." Yet Moor was among those officers who were persuaded to discredit their old captain.

The trip itself was unremarkable. Like Middleton's, it involved a winter far to the south of the main objective, during which company officials showed a hardening hostility toward the interlopers. (The fact that one captain had his wife with him did little to allay company suspicions that Moor was there to give them business competition and not to do any serious exploring.) By the time sailing was resumed in June, the officers were quarreling among themselves, resulting in sluggish progress. When the ships finally reached and explored Wager Inlet, they found, in a crewman's words, that "our hitherto imagined Strait ended in two small unnavigable rivers"—and Dobbs's fond theories were convincingly toppled. It was a humbled and dispirited company that returned to England in October 1747, with little new information and not the slightest evidence to support the obloquy that had been leveled against Middleton.

Popular enthusiasm for the passage waned in the face of all this nega-

Passage seekers in the 18th Century came from east and west. Leaving from Hudson Bay, Samuel Hearne traced the Coppermine River to the Arctic Ocean. Captain James Cook probed the coast of Alaska, penetrated Bering Strait, and was turned back at Icy Cape. And Alexander Mackenzie opened up a river that led to later exploration of the northern coast of Canada.

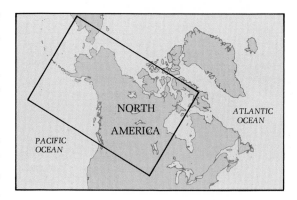

Bold thrusts by river and sea

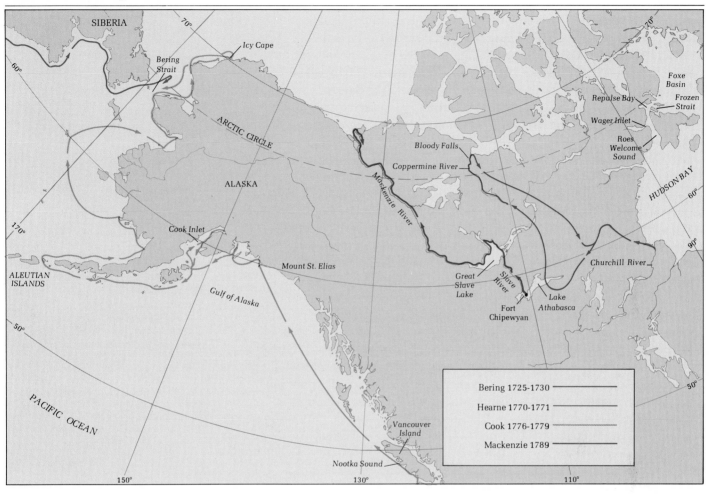

tive evidence, and even Arthur Dobbs discreetly tempered his own zeal in public. Still clinging to his conviction that the Moor voyage had failed because of "the Timidity, ill Conduct or bad Inclination, of some of the Commanders," he began to direct his energy elsewhere; in 1750 he published a paper on "Bees, and the Mode of Taking Wax and Honey." In 1752 he was appointed Governor of North Carolina, in which office he ended his stormy days. He had flared in and out of the story like a comet, and had left behind both the offer of a rich reward and universal doubts that it could ever be won.

Hudson Bay continued to draw explorers for another 30 years, although some of these expeditions were no more than token efforts by the Hudson's Bay Company as advertisement of its professed enthusiasm for discovery. Meanwhile, it was as though informed opinion had pulled back from the problem in order to inspect it from every angle. When the search once more focused down to detail, the object of its attention was no longer the approach from the east. After a long delay, reports of significant Russian discoveries off the far northeastern corner of Asia had filtered back to Europe, suggesting that the current concept of the shape of North America as comparatively narrow at its top was quite erroneous. At the same time, important progress was about to be made on land. These two lines of investigation would demonstrate that Hudson Bay had been a fatal distraction.

The reappraisal was fortified by a dramatic change in the political complexion of North America. In 1763, at the close of the Seven Years' War with France, Britain's possession of Canada was confirmed by the Treaty of Paris. With France virtually eliminated from the competition for an empire in America, Britain's territory now stretched north and south all the way from the Hudson Bay area to the colony of Georgia on the eastern seaboard. But it was imperative, for Britain's imperial designs, that gains on the east coast should be matched in the west. It was here that Britain would come into conflict with the aspirations of two other powers, Russia and Spain.

As far back as 1725 the Danish explorer Vitus Bering, who was then serving as an officer in the Imperial Russian Navy, had started out to determine whether or not Russia was joined to America at the far north of the Pacific Ocean. The journey involved an overland march of some 4,600 miles from St. Petersburg to the Kamchatka Peninsula in Siberia—where Bering constructed two ships with materials he had brought across the long expanse of country. Then he took to the sea. This would have been a sufficiently remarkable achievement for a company of soldiers and sailors; but Bering led a caravan of 570 men with their wives and children, together with a troupe of scientists who insisted on pulling wagonloads of books and instruments.

Bering sailed through the strait that was later given his name, and crossed the Arctic Circle before turning back. Although he did not see the American coast through the thick haze that enshrouded it and did not travel far enough north to rule out the possibility that his strait was a bay, his reports of the journey indicated that a land link between Asia and America was unlikely. On another voyage, in 1741, Bering took his ship east and south of the Aleutian Islands, sighting islands in the Gulf of Alaska and Mount St. Elias on the North American continent. That voyage was his last; he died of scurvy following a shipwreck on an island off the Kamchatka Peninsula.

News that the Russians had reached America alarmed the Spanish, who had presumed sovereignty in the Pacific on the basis of a papal bull in 1493. With nervous urgency Spain dispatched ships northward to forestall any possible Russian claims. By 1774, Spanish vessels had explored the coast as far north as the Queen Charlotte Islands off modern British Columbia. As these developments clarified the real shape of northwestern America, the hypothetical position of the Northwest Passage was pushed farther and farther to the north; and at the same time, the image of its length grew from the short jaunt previously hoped for to a frigid haul of some 2,500 miles. For the first time, the true magnitude of the problem—not only of discovering the passage, but of negotiating it, once found—began to be understood.

The burst of exploration in the Pacific had the additional effect of threatening Britain's prospects for empire. Far from standing idly by,

In this posthumous portrait, Samuel Hearne wears elegant attire at odds with the extraordinary ruggedness he displayed on his trek to the mouth of the Coppermine River in 1771. Fulfilling a boyhood promise to make a name for himself, he took possession of the American Arctic coast on behalf of his employer, the Hudson's Bay Company.

A page from the published journal of Samuel Hearne offers multiple views of a birch-bark canoe used by his Chipewyan Indian guides. Such a canoe, said Hearne, was light enough to be carried on land for miles at a time. One person paddled it through the water, while another could ride in the bottom amid the cargo.

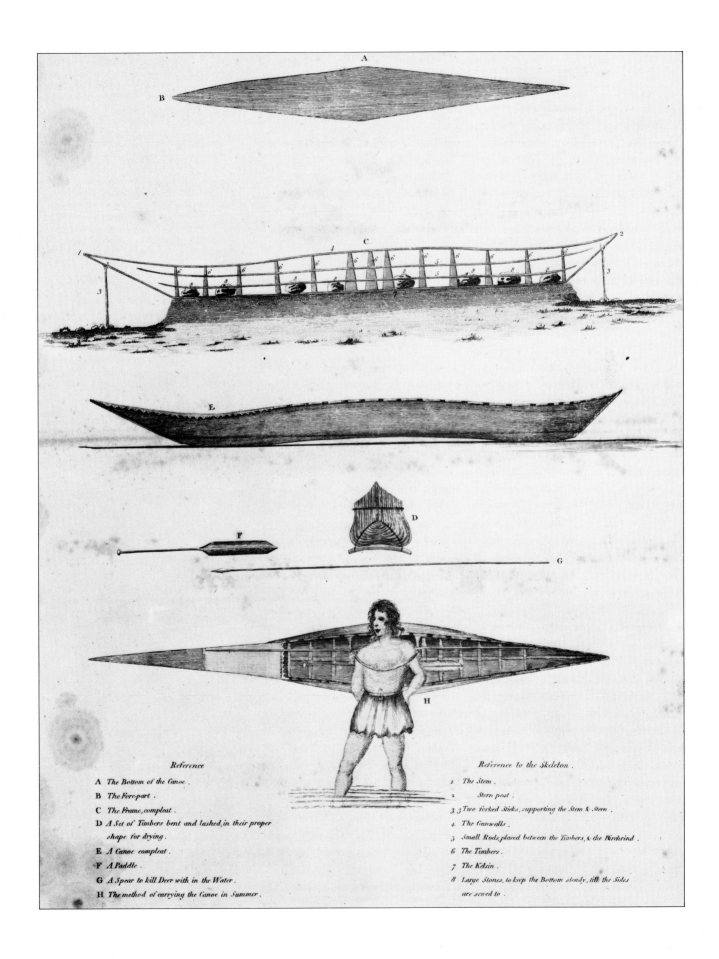

Reference

A The Bottom of the Canoe.

B The Fore-part.

C The Frame, compleat.

D A Set of Timbers bent and lashed, in their proper shape for drying.

E A Canoe compleat.

F A Paddle.

G A Spear to kill Deer with in the Water.

H The method of carrying the Canoe in Summer.

Reference to the Skeleton.

1 The Stem.

2 Stern post.

3 3 Two forked Sticks, supporting the Stem & Stern.

4 The Gunwalls.

5 Small Rods, placed between the Timbers, & the Birchrind.

6 The Timbers.

7 The Kelsin.

8 Large Stones, to keep the Bottom steady, till the Sides are sewed to.

Britain proceeded from two separate directions, east and west. Each thrust was designed to uncover the Northwest Passage; for possession of the passage, together with the annexation of the American coast north of California, would complete an arc of territory that would leave Britain the owner of what was to become modern Canada—and would also give it a connection to the Pacific that could prove of strategic importance in any future quarrel with Spain.

The rejuvenated effort from the east began in November 1769, when Samuel Hearne, a 24-year-old employee of the Hudson's Bay Company, set off cross-country from a fort in the vicinity of Churchill with instructions to locate a river whose banks, according to the Indians, were rich in copper ore—the 15th river that had been part of the geographic vision that drew James Knight to disaster in 1719. Hearne's orders also called for him to follow that river to the sea.

Even among Arctic explorers, Hearne was a man of iron tenacity. He chose Chipewyan Indians for his companions, living entirely on their diet of deer blood and entrails, flesh and skin boiled in fat, and buffalo fetuses ("a great delicacy indeed")—and never contracted scurvy. Despite his determination, a shortage of provisions and the desertions of his Indian guides forced Hearne to give up his first attempt after five weeks. Two months later he was off again—this time to endure injury, cold, hunger and Indian attacks for nine months before his quadrant was smashed by a gust of wind and he was compelled again to return. On his third try, begun in December 1770, he managed to reach a likely river after seven and a half months of tramping across the desolate north. There he witnessed a hideous orgy of bloodshed.

In the last stages of the journey, his party had been joined by a company of high-spirited local Indians who roused the Chipewyans to a cause that was quite different from Hearne's own. Their purpose, they informed him, was to settle an old feud. They had come to kill Eskimos. Hearne protested, but he could not change the minds of these otherwise amiable people. Late one night they found their quarry: a riverside cluster of Eskimo tents lodging some 20 sleeping men, women and children. The Indians crept close, uttered piercing cries and attacked. Hearne "stood neuter in the rear"—until a young Eskimo woman of about 18, a spear piercing her side, fell at his feet, grasped his legs and cried out for mercy. Hearne interceded only enough to persuade the frenzied Indians to put a quick end to her misery. By the time the butchery was finished, no Eskimo in the camp remained alive.

Although he was to be haunted by the killings for years afterward, Hearne pressed on with his assignment. First, he scouted about for the rumored trove of copper. There was none—although the river he was on would be given the name Coppermine in honor of Hearne's quest. Next, he followed the waterway to its mouth. About eight miles beyond the Eskimo camp lay what appeared to be an endless sheet of ice, where families of seals played and rested; closer in, the ice was broken up and the water was dotted with sandbars and islands. Hearne was the first European to view the Arctic Ocean from the American continent. In one sense it was a supremely anticlimactic moment. He had, in his words, "put a final end to all disputes concerning a North West Passage through

Explorers traveling along the Coppermine River in 1821 camp at Bloody Falls, named by Samuel Hearne after he had seen an Indian massacre of Eskimos there 50 years earlier. Many skulls and bones (foreground) remained to identify the spot.

Hudson's Bay." Had there been such a passage, he would have crossed it.

Four years after Hearne's return, Britain authorized the second half of its dual approach to the problem of the passage—a western assault by sea. This probe was entrusted to James Cook, who, at the age of 48, had already compiled an extraordinary record of discovery. He had the unique distinction of having taken possession of an entire continent—Australia—on behalf of his country. He had also sailed around the world twice and had explored more of the Pacific coastline and islands than any man before or after. In the process, by making careful observations and using the newly invented chronometer to determine longitude, Cook had compiled charts whose accuracy would call forth the admiration of generations of mariners.

Moreover, by his attention to scurvy he had transformed the average sailor's experience of the sea from a nightmare to a more bearable, if still risky, way of making a living. For 20 years the Admiralty had been ordering a supply of "roots and Greens to Seamen, with their Fresh Meat," but Cook took the matter further. He insisted on carrying along sauerkraut and grain malt, which contained sufficient vitamin C to prevent the disease—and which would not spoil during the course of a long voyage. As a result, scurvy ceased to be a serious threat, and exploration could become that much more ambitious.

Cook's instructions from the Admiralty showed that Hearne's findings had been taken to heart. He was to sail up the western coast of America to lat. 65°N.—just below the Arctic Circle—before starting his search in earnest; then he was to keep to the coast and explore every inlet, determining whether it cut through to the Arctic Ocean. If not, his orders called for him to follow the shoreline until it turned east toward the outlet of Hearne's Coppermine River and ultimately to its eastern end—wherever that might be.

Simultaneously, a separate expedition set sail from England for Baffin Bay with the purpose of reviving the quest—abandoned since the days of Baffin himself—for an opening out of the western coast of the bay. The commanding officer of this party, however, was hardly of Cook's caliber. Unnerved by the succession of icebergs that towered above his ship ("What to do, I know not," he moaned), Lieutenant Richard Pickersgill had barely touched the coast of Labrador before he "thought it necessary to return" to England.

Cook's expedition left England in two sloops, the 450-ton *Resolution* and the 300-ton *Discovery,* in the summer of 1776. By the following February he had sailed around the Cape of Good Hope, across the southern reaches of the Indian Ocean and into the Pacific. He slowly traversed that ocean's vast expanse, visiting a number of islands—and discovering the Hawaiian Islands in January 1778. From there, he steered north toward a very different realm.

For all his experience, Cook underestimated the adversities of the Arctic, owing to two unfortunate misconceptions. One was an old theory, dating from Tudor times and still popular in some geographical circles, that Arctic ice was formed from the cold water issuing from the rivers of North America and Russia; this implied that if a ship could break through a frozen belt close to land, it would find the polar ocean itself ice-free. The other misconception was based on a map—sanctioned by the St. Petersburg Academy of Sciences and published in 1774—that professed to show the land formations east of Bering Strait. It represented Alaska as an island, separated from the American mainland by a strait on its eastern side. Uncharacteristically credulous, Cook trusted the map—and was to endure weeks of frustration as, approaching the area from the southeast, he probed every inlet in the vain hope of gaining direct access to the northern ocean.

The first American landfall was made in March 1778 on the coast of what is now Oregon. After delays for calking and rerigging and replacing rotten wood on the *Resolution's* masts, the ships stood off the shore below the massive peak of Mount St. Elias, which marks the boundary between Alaska and the Yukon. A mood of expectancy gripped the crews: After two years of island-hopping across the world, they thought their main adventure was ready to begin. But as inlet after inlet proved blind, and the coast continued impenetrably westward and then southwestward, the excitement evaporated.

Later, Cook was to write that the most illiterate of seafaring men "would have been ashamed to put his name to" the map that the Russians had published. At each opening, one or the other vessel sailed in, until the breach grew too shallow or narrow for it to go farther. If any

A Nootka Indian couple of Vancouver Island—where Captain James Cook laid over to refit his vessels in 1778— sport local fashions of braided hair, facial daubing and capes that were woven of cedar bark. The man (top) wears a nose ring of copper; the woman's grass hat is decorated with whaling scenes.

doubts remained, a ship's boat would be sent on alone. All the time, Cook was forced to weigh the need for scrupulous exploration against the advance of the season and the danger that northern waters might ice over before he was able to reach them. By the time he finally arrived at Bering Strait, he had established beyond doubt that this was the only northern exit from the Pacific.

It was now August 9, much later than he had planned. Still, if the ice proved to be no more than a narrow belt, as the experts predicted, he should be able to get through—although breaking out at the eastern end might prove a more formidable task. The ships moved confidently north and northeast. Then, on August 17, came disillusionment. For some days the men had noticed what Cook described as a "sharpness of the air and gloomyness of the weather." Now they "perceived a brightness in the Northern horizon like that reflected from ice, commonly called the blink." The ships were approaching a great barrier of ice, 10 to 12 feet high at its edge and stretching ahead as far as the eye could see. This was manifestly not the frozen effluent from rivers, but an endless carpet blocking all progress. Once again the academic theorists had been proved wrong by arduous experience.

Hugging the shore, the ships reached and named Alaska's Icy Cape, some 300 miles beyond Bering Strait; but it was obvious that if they attempted to push on they would run the risk of being crushed between the coast and the advancing ice wall. So Cook turned away—following the ice wall to the Asian coast to make sure there was no opening in the barrier it presented—and then slipped down through Bering Strait to a more moderate climate.

It was Cook's intention to return the following year and forge beyond Icy Cape. But while spending the winter in the Hawaiian islands, he was killed by Polynesians in a squabble that stemmed from some minor pilfering. He had nevertheless pioneered the route that would give his successors a decisive advantage in future western assaults on the passage. Cook had charted the northern American coastline more completely and accurately than ever before; he had exploded the hokum about polar ice and the layout of the North Pacific; and he had provided an example of seamanship that would strongly influence the more professional navy of the next century.

Cook's death held a special irony. If he had been a month earlier in his attempt and had passed Point Barrow, where the coastline turns away toward the east and the Canadian archipelago, neither he nor his men—given the state of their supplies and the strength of the vessels—would have come out alive. Within two or three weeks they would have found themselves imprisoned in an icy tomb from which escape would have been impossible.

Now that Cook had ruled out the possibility of a passage in the more southerly latitudes of America's Pacific coast, and with the discovery of the Coppermine River, another mystery arose—one concerning the interior geography of Canada. Since the early days of the Hudson's Bay Company, traders and adventurers had located a number of rivers meandering through the northlands. Cook had proved that these rivers did not

empty into the Pacific; and it was impossible that such immense quantities of water could feed into the shallow Coppermine before reaching the Arctic. Where, then, did the rivers lead?

The challenge was taken up by a young Scottish fur trader named Alexander Mackenzie, an employee of the North West Company—the Hudson's Bay Company's first major competitor. On the basis of Indian tales and speculative maps, Mackenzie postulated the existence of an undiscovered river fed by a multitude of tributaries. In June 1789 he set out from Fort Chipewyan—located on Lake Athabasca in present-day Alberta—with four large canoes, a crew of the French-Canadian trappers called voyageurs, and several Indian guides and interpreters, one of whom had served with Hearne's expedition. Six days of arduous paddling down the Slave River brought them to the Great Slave Lake. His guides picked up information that this large body of water gave rise to a mighty river at its western end. Four days later Mackenzie had located the passage and started down it.

Indians they encountered along the river banks offered them horrific descriptions of the river's length and treachery. Mackenzie remembered their warning that "we all should be old Men by the time we would return," and that the explorers "would have to encounter many Monsters." As it turned out, the only menace they had to fight off was "being nearly suffocated by Swarms of Musquittoes." Paddling the large canoes as much as 100 miles a day, the expedition followed the broad, swift waterway all the way to the Arctic Ocean by mid-July. There they found a dismaying vista of pack ice that extended to the horizon. Mackenzie stayed only long enough to take note of the action of the tides and take navigational sightings. He then retraced his route back up the great river that would bear his name.

In all, Mackenzie covered more than 2,000 miles in just 102 days—a phenomenal pace. The 25-year-old Scotsman had opened up territory that would yield a stupendous bounty in furs, and he had identified the outlet for a number of the rivers wandering across the Canadian north. But once again discovery had brought disappointment: Like Samuel Hearne and Captain Cook before him, he had found no northwest passage on his way to the Arctic.

The tribulations and triumphs of the 18th Century thus marked a new epoch in the search for the Northwest Passage. A southerly channel had been excluded as a possibility, and it was evident that a northern route would be difficult at best, a deadly ordeal at worst. When the search was taken up once again, after the long hiatus of the Napoleonic Wars, commerce was no longer a consideration. The Northwest Passage was to be a challenge to a new breed, a breed whose impetus came from the excitement of sheer physical endeavor, from a desire to fill in the empty blanks in the world's map, and from a thirst for knowledge simply for knowledge's sake. The age of myth was over.

Captain Cook's ships, the Resolution and the Discovery, are beset by an advancing ice field near Icy Cape, Alaska. They narrowly escaped by tacking southwest through the only opening in the floes.

Stratagems in the struggle against ice

Mariners who ventured into the Arctic to probe for the Northwest Passage battled constantly with the elements, but nothing posed such an impediment to ships—or so tested the determination of the crews—as did ice. From about October to June, the waters in the area of search were frozen solid. In July, however, the polar cap began to crack apart into jagged floes, and it was then that Arctic adventurers—typified here and on the following pages by an early 19th Century expedition—attempted the passage.

When the winds were unfavorable or channels too narrow or tortuous for safe maneuvering, the explorers themselves moved the ship, either towing it or manning the capstan to reel in ice grapnels planted ahead. Vigilance could not be relaxed for a moment, since winds, currents or tides could send a massive floe or a whole ice pack bearing down on the ship. If the men could not maneuver clear of the danger, they moved the vessel into a cranny inside stationary ice along a shore and prayed that it would act as a buffer.

In September a thin layer of ice began to form on the water, knitting the channels together. The men piled on sail and plowed the ship through this crystalline skin, but inevitably there came a moment when, as one captain wrote, nature drew "the boundary which we were not to pass."

Then the explorers retreated to a sheltered anchorage near shore to spend the winter. When the sun finally began to melt the ice again, the voyagers would speed the release with saws, chisels and round-the-clock labor, for even an extra day of sailing in the brief summer might make the difference between completing their mission that year or spending another winter in the Arctic's frozen manacles.

Investigating the channel ahead of the ship, a crewman dredges up samples of the bottom; the material might indicate a current and thus a link with a larger body of water. One of his fellows, standing beside him, takes the water's temperature to judge how close it is to freezing. A third man leans over the rail to release a bottle containing the ship's bearings; if the ship fails to return home on time, the floating message might help guide a rescue expedition. In the background, men in another boat chip off pieces of land ice, which will be melted and used for drinking water.

As members of her crew strain at the capstan to take up a hawser that has been attached to the ice, the exploration vessel inches her way around a floe.

Standing on the floe, three men chip away projections of ice that could damage the rigging as the vessel passes by. Men in the boat nearby attach a second hawser to the ice by means of an ice grapnel. And around the bend, another work party takes soundings to find the safest course for the ship to follow.

Racing against time to prevent their vessel from being crushed by an enormous, wind-driven floe that is approaching from the port side, crewmen use gunpowder in order to blast open a safer mooring in the stationary shore ice.

Three men rock their skiff from side to side to break up a layer of thin ice that has formed in front of the exploration vessel, while the crew in the boat to the left attacks the ice with poles and chisels. Since the wind has died for the moment, two other boats tow the vessel through the cleared passage. "When the sheet has acquired a thickness of about half an inch," one explorer wrote, "a ship is liable to be stopped by it"—even when there is a favorable breeze in her sails. He added that a vessel caught in this helpless condition "has often reminded me of Gulliver tied down by the feeble hands of Lilliputians."

The kneeling crewman in the foreground prepares an additional charge as he pours gunpowder into an empty meat cannister. The man at right stirs tallow, which is used to seal the container after a fuse has been inserted.

At the vessel's stern, members of the crew remove the rudder before the ship is backed into her berth—a position that will allow the reinforced bow of the vessel to bear the brunt of the pressure when the approaching ice closes in.

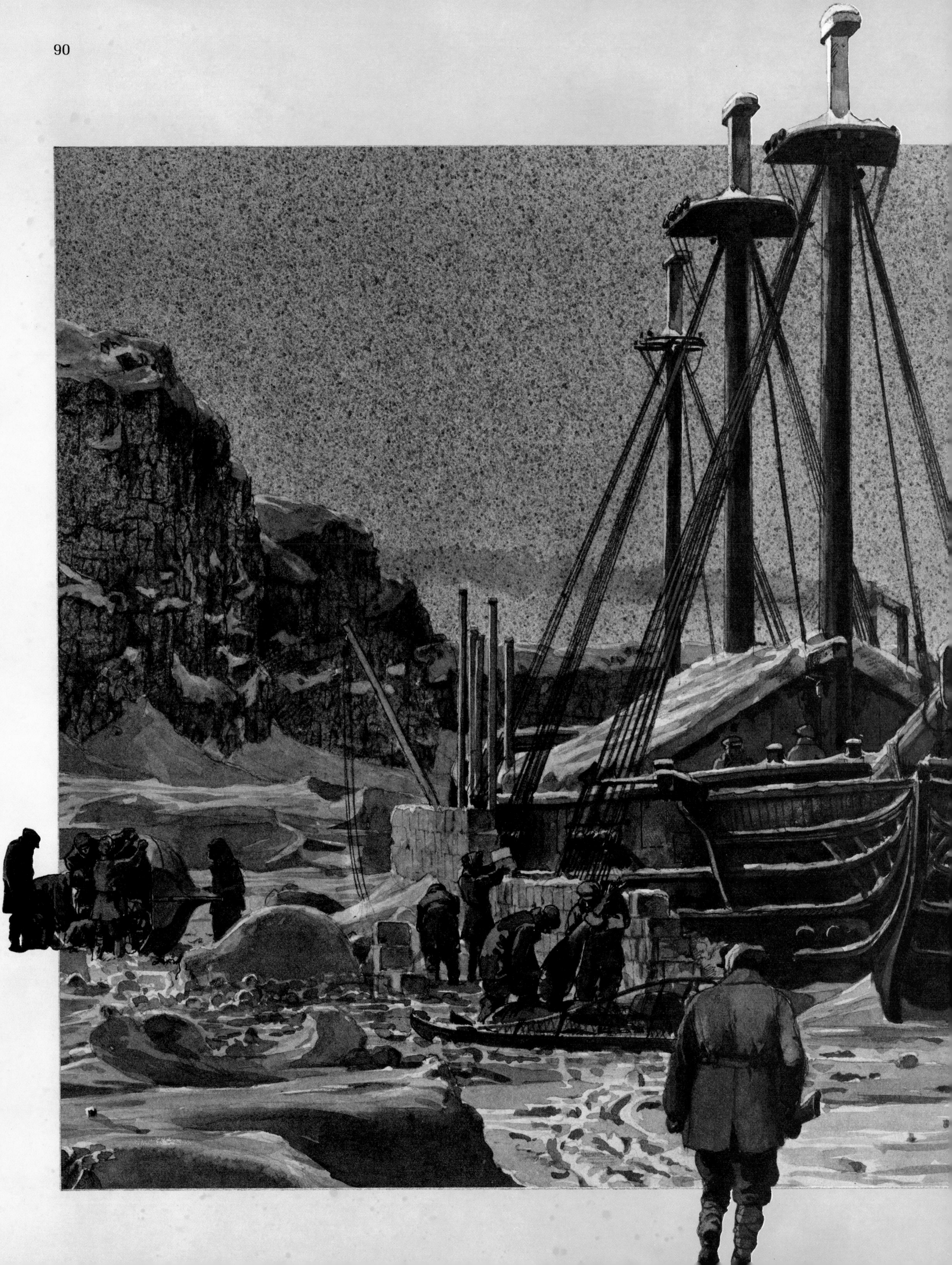

Perched on a ladder, a crewman lays the last section of canvas roofing over the upper deck to create a place for exercise in inclement weather. Others fill lanterns, tidy storage areas and calk a hatchway. After all these tasks were completed, a layer of ice and snow—sprinkled with sand for better traction—was spread on the upper deck to serve as insulation and reduce the loss of heat from the living quarters below.

After blasting their way through shore ice to a sheltered anchorage near land, the explorers complete their preparations for the winter months. To provide extra living space, the upper deck has been roofed in, and men are stowing little-used supplies outside the ship under the boats (far left). Others labor at building a wall of ice and snow around the hull to help insulate the ship from wind and cold. Meanwhile, a hunting party unloads seal carcasses—high in calories, and therefore a useful dietary supplement—from a sledge; the meat's content of vitamin C also helped in the prevention of scurvy.

With the return of warmer weather the explorers chop trenches all around the vessel, to release her from the foot or two of ice that remains. Under the stern, members of the crew attack the ice with chisels and a long saw. Along the sides of the ship, men have rigged up systems of pulleys that raise the saw blades after each downward stroke. On the starboard quarter, another team uses the vessel's davits to hoist out the blocks of ice that have been sawed free.

Aided by a blade-lifting pulley system, a crew saws a canal from open water back to the vessel, following a route that has been sounded and marked out with boarding pikes. In the foreground, crewmen use a hawser to drag a section of detached ice out of the canal. The men working behind them, taking advantage of a favorable breeze, have fitted a larger piece with a mast and sail to float it clear.

Trudging along the sides of the canal, crewmen haul the vessel out to open water. Ahead, others work in boats to break up ice that continues to form. "Nothing could exceed the alacrity" with which the men accomplished their release, one captain wrote, explaining that the prospect of getting under way again "was to persons cooped up as we had been, exhilarating almost beyond conception."

Chapter 4

Inside the maze

uring the early years of the 19th Century, the English were preoccupied with holding Napoleon at bay and had little energy to spare for their affair with the Arctic. Then, like a coquette who is surprised to find that her playful discouragement of her suitors has been taken too seriously, the Arctic began to flirt once more. Suddenly the stubborn front she had always presented to aspiring conquerors quite literally melted. In the summer of 1817, an English whaling captain named William Scoresby reported that nearly 18,000 square miles of pack ice between Greenland and Spitsbergen had disappeared. Scoresby also observed a phenomenon that he considered to be definitive proof of a northern waterway linking the Atlantic with the Pacific. His crews had caught whales in both oceans—and had found, embedded in their blubber, harpoons the men recognized as characteristic of whalers from the opposite sea. There could thus be no doubt of the existence of a sea-lane open at least to whales, and it seemed only logical that the sharp warming trend and the clearance of ice would open the passage to ships as well.

Scoresby's opinions soon found their way to John Barrow, Second Secretary of the Admiralty and influential heir to Arthur Dobbs's passionate belief in the Northwest Passage. Tireless, obdurate and dogmatic, he had been granted his Admiralty post in 1803, when he was in his late thirties, and he would serve in that position for four decades. Like Dobbs, Barrow could be unscrupulous and vicious. During his years of near-absolute rule over the Royal Navy, things did not often go smoothly for anyone who tried to thwart his aims, whether or not the opponent was in the right.

Although the commercial allure of the Northwest Passage had faded away, there were plenty of other reasons for continuing the quest. Scholars desired more and better information about the Arctic, and statesmen agreed that the discovery of a passage would add luster to the image of Britain as the world's preeminent sea power. Barrow himself wrote a book detailing the history of northwest exploration and published a lengthy article in a respected English journal, the *Quarterly Review*, extolling the search as in "every way worthy of a great and prosperous and enlightened nation; having for its primary object that of the advancement of science, for its own sake."

After hearing Scoresby's reports, Barrow presented the Admiralty with a scheme for a two-fold effort in the Arctic: One expedition, proceeding through Davis Strait, would resume the hunt for a channel through the North American continent; the other, taking advantage of the thaw, would head due north into the Arctic Ocean. Shortly after he announced his plans, Parliament established a new system of financial

In an engraving based on a sketch by Captain John Ross, a polar bear leaps into Davis Strait after coming under fire from a shipboard marksman. The incident occurred in September 1818, during a voyage that would make Ross the most controversial figure in Arctic exploration.

rewards for Arctic explorations (and stipulated that Navy ships were eligible). In appreciation of the magnitude of the undertaking, a sliding scale of prizes was introduced: A sum of £5,000 would be awarded to the first ship to pass long. 110° W.; £10,000 to the first to pass 130° W.; £15,000 to the first to pass 150° W.; and £20,000 to the ship's company that first reached the Pacific.

Barrow's North Pole expedition failed even before it could become clear that his assumptions concerning melted polar ice were completely wrongheaded: A violent gale off Spitsbergen sent his polar explorers scurrying back home. However, the northwest effort, under the command of a sturdy and resourceful Scot named John Ross, would prove to be more successful.

Ross had studied the experiences of the 18th Century explorers and had learned his lessons well. He hand-picked his crews and had his two ships—the 385-ton converted whaler *Isabella* and the 252-ton *Alexander*—clad inside and out with extra timbers and iron to help them lunge through ice and resist the pressure that would be exerted on the hulls if they became icebound during the winter. He packed the ships with axes, saws, spurs, hooks, poles, anchors and boats—all specially designed for use in the ice. To win over the Eskimos, he brought along plenty of alcohol, firearms and knickknacks, including 40 umbrellas—perfectly useless in the Arctic, but likely to appeal to the local people as a novelty, he thought.

The expedition set sail on April 18, 1818, and by the beginning of June it was skirting the west coast of Greenland, putting into land only to carry out scientific observations. Sometimes the going was hazardous. The melting ice released icebergs that could reach cathedral dimensions, and moving floes occasionally pushed the ships against the shore, causing the vessels' bottoms to grind against the sea floor. But even when the ice impeded the progress of the expedition, the explorers retained their good humor. At one point, the entire crew of the *Isabella* debarked onto pack ice and, using a line tied to the foremast head, themselves pulled the ship along to the accompaniment of marching tunes that were provided by a fiddler.

As they rounded Cape York, where Baffin Bay turns into its northernmost narrows, they were amazed to observe that the snow on the cliffs and slopes was deep crimson; later, scientists would discover that a bed of algae was responsible for the tint. In this region they met a tribe of Eskimos who had never before seen Europeans, much less a sailing ship. Primed by an Eskimo guide they had brought along, His Britannic Majesty's officers all pulled their noses as a gesture of friendship. The Eskimos, torn between fear and curiosity, were slowly reassured by smiles, gestures and the offer of knives and looking glasses. It was the latter, according to Ross, that at last softened the Eskimos' reserve: "On seeing their faces in the glasses," he wrote, "their astonishment appeared extreme, and they looked round in silence, for a moment, at each

Swaths of crimson snow along an eight-mile stretch of Greenland cliffs so intrigued John Ross during his 1818 expedition that he sent men ashore to investigate. They were not able to solve the mystery, because the cause was microscopic—a single-celled plant, Chlamydomonas nivalis, that flourishes under cold and wet conditions.

Towering peaks, named Croker's
Mountains by John Ross in honor of the
First Secretary of the Admiralty,
appear to obstruct Lancaster Sound. Ross
sighted and sketched the obstacle after
penetrating 80 miles into the channel. A
year later, he learned that the looming
range had in fact been a mirage.

other and at us; immediately afterwards they set up a general shout, succeeded by a loud laugh, expressive of extreme delight, as well as surprise, in which we joined."

From then on, with considerable innocent misunderstanding, laughter and obligatory nose-pulling, everything went well. The Eskimos, thinking that the vessels' sails were a form of wings, addressed the ships as living creatures. "Who are you?" they asked. "What are you? Where do you come from? Is it from the sun or the moon?" For their part, the Englishmen were delighted with the Eskimos' merriment and with their gifts of bone knives, narwhal horns and walrus tusks, which the explorers called sea-horse teeth.

Late in August the ships reached their northernmost point, Whale Sound. Ahead, in Smith Sound, lay solid ice. More than a century earlier, Baffin had come this far and had also been halted by ice. He had come to the conclusion that no passage was to be found in the area; but Ross, who now crossed to the shore opposite Greenland and followed it southward, remained hopeful. The first large inlet he encountered, Jones Sound, was choked by ice, and he wrote it off as a bay. Then on September 1, a hundred miles farther on, the explorers saw the coastline fall back into the broad sweep of Lancaster Sound. Forty-five miles from cape to cape and bounded by tall, snow-clad mountains, the inlet was certainly inviting, and men crowded the crow's-nest and masthead to scan the horizon for signs of the long-sought passage. But Ross knew that Baffin had determined that this too was a blind bay; and according to his later account of the journey, Ross found much that supported his predecessor's conclusion. There was neither current nor swell from the west, and the water around the ships became colder, indicating a flow off the land rather than from the sea.

Just to be sure, Ross continued his probe almost 100 miles into the sound. Patches of fog obscured the view, but a clearing during the morning watch enabled Ross to see "a high ridge of mountains, extending directly across the bottom of the inlet." Even so, "I was determined completely to explore it," he stated, "and, therefore, continued all sail." In midafternoon he was interrupted at his dinner by an officer of the watch, who came to report that the fog was lifting. Hurrying topside, he "distinctly saw the land, round the bottom of the bay, forming a connected chain of mountains with those which extended along the north and south sides." He named the range Croker's Mountains, after the First Secretary of the Admiralty. Again the fog closed in, but by now Ross was convinced that more effort would only be wasted. He signaled the *Alexander* to follow, and turned about.

Ross concluded the expedition with a diligent survey of Baffin Bay, and then crossed Davis Strait and stood for home at the end of September. He had lost no men to sickness, nor had cause to punish anyone. He commended many of his officers with generosity. Back home, he augmented his judgments with a solid body of scientific observations: charts, compass bearings, and notes he had made on atmospheric electricity and the specific gravity and temperature of sea water in different latitudes. He was an exemplary commander. But Ross was soon to suffer the galling knowledge that, in the uncertain visibility of Lancaster

The return of the disappointing Ross expedition is cruelly ridiculed in this 1819 cartoon. A porcine Ross struts at the head of his crew—all apparently rendered noseless by excessive nose-pulling, the popular greeting of Eskimos. The captain's nephew, James Clark Ross, holds on to the front paws of a polar bear while astronomer Edward Sabine, an army captain, hoists a bayoneted gull. A grotesque Eskimo brings up the rear.

Sound, he had committed a disastrous mistake—one that all but destroyed his reputation.

Like many men of forthright views, Ross had enemies. One of them was certainly John Barrow. Although there was nothing at the time to prove that Ross had made an error (he was even promoted to the rank of post captain two months after he had returned), Barrow still believed in the Northwest Passage and was certain that Ross had somehow failed to find it. In the pages of the *Quarterly Review*, he blasted Ross's conclusions. Within a year Barrow saw to it that the search was resumed—again by two expeditions.

The task of one was to follow the overland route pioneered by Samuel Hearne in 1771, and then to explore the coast of what Barrow expected to be the central stretch of the Northwest Passage. This campaign was led by a 33-year-old lieutenant, John Franklin, who had served honorably in the Napoleonic Wars and had tasted Arctic life the previous year on the abortive attempt to enter the Arctic Ocean.

The second expedition, more offensive to Ross's dignity, was to follow his own route of the year before. Ignoring his denial that there was any outlet from Baffin Bay, the expedition was to examine more carefully the possibilities of passing through Lancaster Sound or, failing that, through Jones or Smith Sounds. Command was given to a young man, William Edward Parry, who had served under Ross as commander of the *Alexander* and had received generous praise from Ross for his service. Parry had not reciprocated: He was convinced that Ross had given up the probe of Lancaster Sound too early—although he had no proof that the mountainous obstacle spotted by Ross did not exist, since his own vessel was lagging far behind the *Isabella* at the time. Others agreed with Parry. It must have aggrieved Ross further to know that several of the officers who now accompanied Parry had served with Ross the year before and owed much of their success to his meticulous example—including his nephew James Clark Ross.

Parry had everything going for him when he started out on May 11, 1819. The weather was propitious, and his two ships—the 375-ton bomb vessel *Hecla* and the 180-ton gun brig *Griper*—were equipped with sufficient provisions to last for two winters. They reached the mouth of Lancaster Sound on August 1, having taken a full month less than Ross had. The ice barrier at the entrance was negligible, and a brisk wind was blowing from the east—perfect conditions for resolving the rival claims of Ross and Barrow.

"It is more easy," wrote Parry, "to imagine than describe the almost breathless anxiety which was now visible on every countenance." Soon the ships had passed the point where Ross had erected a flag to mark his farthest attainment. On both sides the coast rose up to jagged white peaks; but ahead there was nothing but clear water—no mountain barrier. The mythical Croker's Mountains had been demolished for good, and Parry was free to proceed where no European had ever sailed before. Barrow's armchair topography had proved accurate.

Still, Ross's vanishing mountains were not the "pitiable excuse for running away home" that Barrow had charged. Ross had believed they were there—and had gone so far as to draw a picture of them—but

*Holding a telescope in one hand and
wearing a heavy Arctic glove on the other,
William Parry is the very image of
the polar adventurer in this 1820 portrait.
Parry became the toast of England for
his bold thrust through Lancaster Sound
and his subsequent sweep 600 miles
across the top of North America.*

he had been the victim of a mirage, a trick of Arctic refraction. What appeared to him to be a range of peaks in Lancaster Sound could only have been fields of broken ice that had been raised by an optical illusion to the dimensions of mountains.

A sharp gale rising from the east sped Parry's progress through the uncharted waters. Crewmen began to calculate the likely distance to Cook's Icy Cape and to look forward to the day when they would bask in the balmier climes of the Pacific. In early August they came upon a body of land that Parry named North Somerset, after the county in England where he was born; it is now known as Somerset Island. He turned southward and followed the island's east coast for 120 miles, until ice blocked the way. Parry believed that these waters—which he named Prince Regent Inlet—connected with Hudson Bay, and he was convinced that it was possible to breach the ice. But right now he was in too much of a hurry. He retraced his route to Lancaster Sound and then proceeded westward.

Luck continued to favor him. There was no letup in the thaw, and he wrote that "the same part of the sea which but a day or two before had been completely covered with floes to the utmost extent of view" was now an open passage. As the ships passed islands and inlets on all sides, Parry bestowed names with the largesse of a conquering general: Wellington Channel, Cornwallis, Griffith, Bathurst, Byam Martin, and Melville Islands and Barrow Strait (as a testimonial of his "esteem for that gentleman and as a public acknowledgment due to him for his zeal and exertions"). On September 4, when the explorers were halfway to Bering Strait and almost at the meridian of the mouth of Hearne's Coppermine River, they crossed long. 110° W., an achievement that earned the voyagers a Parliamentary prize—£5,000, to be divided among the crews. Beer and an increased ration of meat cheered the men's evening meal, and a nearby headland of Melville Island was christened Bounty Cape in celebration.

But this amazing progress was nearing its end. As the coast curved away to the northwest, the ice—a continuation of the permanent sheet over the Beaufort Sea—proved immovably hard. At 112° 51' W., Parry gave orders to turn back to a harbor already sighted on the southeast coast of Melville Island. There, the men covered the upper decks of the *Hecla* with a sturdy canvas roof and created as much comfort as they could for the months ahead.

An eerie silence descended. "The sound of voices," wrote Parry, "which, in the calm and cold air, was heard at an extraordinary distance, alone broke the deathlike stillness that reigned around." The brilliant dazzle of sunlit ice darkened to a gloaming pallor as, in early November, the sun set for the last time in three months. The temperature dropped steadily: By January it hovered between 30° and 40° below zero F., and on one occasion, in February, it plummeted to −55°. The steam from cooking and the moisture from the men's breath condensed in beads on the walls of the *Hecla*.

To pass the hours, the men amused themselves with such diversions as sing-a-longs (to the strains of a portable organ) and amateur theatricals. The plays chosen were popular farces of the day, made even more rollicking by the officers who took on the female roles—wearing dainty costumes that exposed them to a nasty chill as well as to the ribald wisecracks of their comrades. The crewmen also printed a newspaper, *The North Georgia Gazette and Winter Chronicle,* with contributions by the likes of Sir Pitiful Punster and Frosticus.

The end of April saw the return of migratory birds and animals, giving the men a chance to restock their supplies of fresh meat. In June, Parry led a sledge expedition across Melville Island, and at one point bored through 14 feet of ice and determined—by taste—that sea water, rather than the fresh water of a lake, lay below. Not until August did the sun again release the ships.

Proceeding south, Parry soon realized that the expedition had reached its limit. The explorers sighted a shadowy coastline (which Parry named Banks Land after the president of the Royal Society), but they were blocked from approaching it. Parry called a brief council with his officers, and all agreed that the ice barrier to the west made further exploration impossible. By November 3, 1820, they were back in England, to the rapturous acclaim of their sponsors and the public. Only John Ross had reason for despondence. Parry's success was irrefutable evidence that Ross had not only erred but had missed his own chance for glory. Ross, however, was no man to mope. He vigorously defended himself against the many attacks on his judgment.

Parry had now made the most extensive addition to the map of the American Arctic since the voyage of Baffin himself. He had tried his key in a lock that few thought existed, and the door had opened, offering him 600 miles of unimpeded progress from the entrance of Lancaster Sound to the cove on Melville Island, now named Winter Harbor. But one sober fact stood out: At the end of that path there lay a frozen rampart that no ship could breach.

Still backed by Barrow, Parry was anxious to follow up his achievement with a new expedition. This time he decided to give the northern extremities of Hudson Bay one more chance and ignore what seemed like the false, if beguiling, promise of Lancaster Sound. It was, after all, just possible that the recent trend toward a more benign climate might offer opportunities that had been denied to the explorers of the past. Perhaps the forbidding sheet of ice that covered Foxe Basin had yielded to reveal a passage north of Repulse Bay and Frozen Strait, leading to the southern end of Prince Regent Inlet. It was possible, too, that at a more southerly latitude the western coast of the inlet might offer direct access to the open sea.

Parry sailed again in May 1821, just six months after he had returned to England. For his second expedition he chose the *Hecla* once more, along with an identical bomb vessel, the *Fury*—thus ensuring a supply of interchangeable spare parts in the event of an emergency. His first aim was to clear up, once and for all, the controversy concerning Frozen Strait and Repulse Bay, which had been simmering ever since the pugnacious Arthur Dobbs had first questioned the findings of Christopher Middleton 79 years earlier. After a false start to the south, Parry found Frozen Strait—and was able to get through. Penetrating to Re-

An unusual piece of equipment aboard Parry's flagship Hecla was this barrel organ; it provided 40 tunes, ranging from hymns to reels, for the entertainment of the members of the icebound expedition during the winter of 1819-1820.

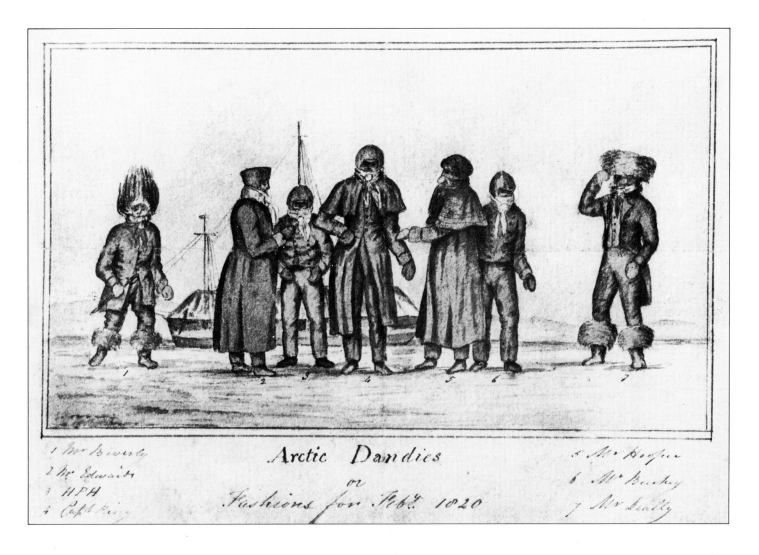

Arctic Dandies

or

Fashions for Feby 1820

Bundled up against the cold, Captain Parry (center) and his "Arctic Dandies" take their daily constitutional near one of the expedition's ice-gripped ships on February 4, 1820—a day when the temperature was recorded at –38°F.

pulse Bay, he was rewarded with the confirmation that Middleton had been correct, after all: There was no passage out of the bay, either to the west or to the north.

Having vindicated Middleton, Parry carried the search northward. The two ships ended that year's voyaging beside Winter Island, off the west coast of Foxe Basin. Here the long wait was enlivened by the presence of a settlement of Eskimos, who drew maps indicating that the polar ocean might be reached the next spring (although they could not assess the chances of a 400-ton ship making it through). The Eskimos' concepts of time and space were nothing at all like English notions: They measured distances in "sleeps," or the number of nights spent on the journey, which naturally varied widely with the weather and the expertise of the travelers. But their skill in coping with their hibernal environment nevertheless called forth the seamen's admiration—particularly their deft use of snow and ice to fashion their domed houses, wolf traps and even dog sledges. Some of these indigenous people enchanted the explorers with their attempts to adopt the manners of the Englishmen —contemptuously dropping stray insects into the fire, for instance, instead of munching on them.

A heartening burst of progress

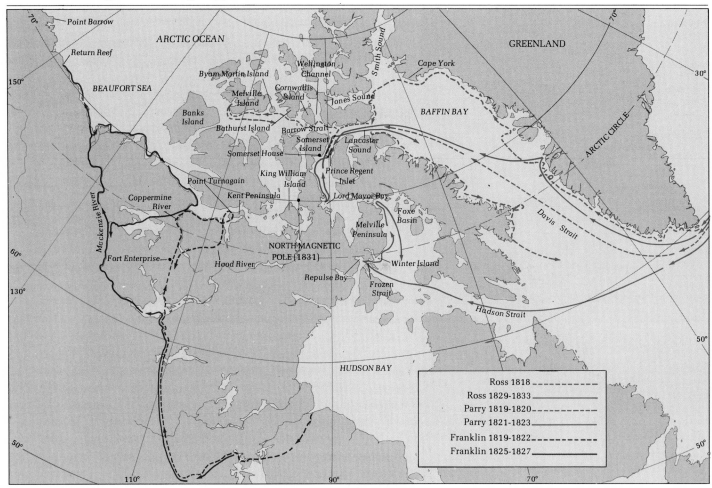

With the welcome arrival of summer, Parry decided to investigate the Eskimos' story of a channel to the north. It was no easy task. Simply to break loose from their winter quarters involved 18 days of hacking a channel through four-foot-thick ice, and the explorers were to confront worse problems farther north. Ice bore down on them with such rapidity that one floe, barely missing a collision with the *Fury*, struck another mass of ice with a violence that shot chunks of ice 60 feet into the air. When the men finally reached the promised strait, they found it stifled from end to end with solid ice. They waited for a clearance, but a second winter descended without any significant change. Hoping to stave off scurvy, Parry planted a miniature crop of watercress and mustard greens in a box of soil he had brought from England. When the disease did break out, it was only among those men who had refused their salads and lime juice, and it was quickly cured. Nevertheless, realizing that the main food stores would not last another winter, Parry started for home. The channel, which he called the Strait of Fury and Hecla, would later be shown to link with the southern extension of Prince Regent Inlet. But as far as Parry was concerned, it might as well have been land.

Parry returned to England this time to discover that he had competition for the Admiralty's plaudits. The new hero of the search for the passage was John Franklin, who had completed three harrowing years of overland exploration in the hinterland and along the central section of the coast of northern Canada.

Franklin had started out in September 1819 from a trading post that was located on the western shore of Hudson Bay, with instructions to follow a line of rivers and lakes to the upper reaches of Hearne's Coppermine River, and then to retrace Hearne's route to the mouth of the river. There Franklin was to move out to sea by canoe and chart the coastline to the east. Franklin's party comprised a much-traveled Scottish naval surgeon, John Richardson; two young midshipmen, Robert Hood and George Back; and a few seamen.

The territory covered during the first winter had been well mapped through the earlier activities of the Hudson's Bay Company and the Northwest Company, and was speckled at distant intervals with trading posts where the explorers could rest and refresh themselves. The traders lent them equipment, including a sledge with a team of dogs, and boats for navigating the rivers and lakes when ice allowed. Along the way, Franklin was able to hire a motley company of 17 French-Canadian *voyageurs* to serve as boatmen and hunters; he also signed on some Indian men and women to work as paid guides.

By the late summer of 1820, a year after their departure, Franklin and his party had traversed some 2,000 miles and were ready to prepare themselves to spend a second winter. Franklin selected a point they named Fort Enterprise, not far from the source of the Coppermine River. From a hut constructed of such substantial wood as they were able to find, the men ventured out to hunt reindeer—most birds having migrated south for the winter—and laid up a stock of 180. Then, with nothing left to do, the men lapsed into a winter lethargy. With the temperature in the hut dropping down to 40° below zero before the fires were lighted in the morning, equipment like chronometers and compasses ceased to function. Franklin and the other officers passed many of their waking hours reading devout books, and many more in soothing the Indians' fears about being murdered or enslaved by hostile tribes.

May brought relief and renewed energy. Bilberries and cranberries abounded, and small birds began to return. By the beginning of June the party was ready to move on. Franklin reflected that the name Fort Enterprise might "with great and deplorable propriety, be changed to that of the 'House of Misery, Lamentation, and Woe.' " In spite of this judgment, he intended to winter again in Fort Enterprise after completing his exploratory assignment. A clerk of the Northwest Company and some local Indians promised to provision the hut with stores before Franklin's company came back.

For the next three weeks the men descended the river, coursing over violent rapids and through defiles flanked by rocky cliffs as much as 100 feet high. At the end of July they reached the sea, and without delay embarked in their two canoes—vessels unsuited to the winds, waves and storms that would harass them. A number of the *voyageurs*, growing fainthearted at the sight of ocean swells, tried to turn back; in the end

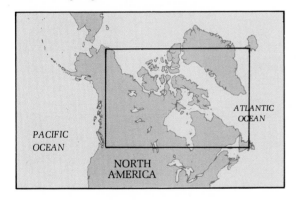

British interest in the Northwest Passage intensified in the early 19th Century. While John Franklin started from inland bases to map the coast from Return Reef to Point Turnagain, John Ross and William Parry made dramatic penetrations of the Arctic archipelago via Lancaster Sound.

they obeyed Franklin's orders, but not without grumbling. They were later suspected of pilfering food, something the expedition could ill afford. Bags of pemmican (a concoction of pounded deer meat and suet, dried according to an Indian recipe) had become wet and turned bad, and beef Franklin had brought from England proved so poorly cured that it was now rancid. The Eskimos had said there would be seals in plenty. There were—but they stayed cannily out of reach. One brown bear was shot, but the *voyageurs* refused to touch it because its flesh appeared diseased. Undaunted, the Englishmen salvaged the paws and ate them boiled. They even improvised "swamp tea" out of an Indian plant that smelled, they thought, like rhubarb.

Considering the conditions, the progress they made was magnificent. In 28 days they charted 550 miles of coast east of the Coppermine estuary. But by the end of August, having sighted no Eskimos with whom to barter for food, Franklin knew that their only hope lay in returning as swiftly as possible. He had reached the north side of what was later called Kent Peninsula. Giving his farthest achievement the descriptive name of Point Turnagain, he decided to strike inland from a nearby estuary, making a triangle of the whole journey.

The party now headed southwest and struggled up a river that Franklin named after Midshipman Hood. The going was rough, with snow and gale-force winds hampering their progress. During a portage, one of the canoes was demolished—deliberately, Franklin thought—by a *voyageur* who said he had stumbled over some rocks. At least it provided fuel for a campfire. A few days later the *voyageurs* announced that they had dumped the remaining canoe because it also was too damaged to be of further use.

This presented a problem the next time the party encountered a river. The *voyageurs* contrived a flimsy, one-man raft out of dwarf willow branches. For it to be useful, however, someone had to get across the water first, carrying a rope to set up a ferry system. In spite of the weakness that assailed him, Dr. Richardson volunteered to swim to the other side. He got two thirds of the way across the river before his limbs went numb in the near-freezing water and he began to sink. Fortunately, he was tied to the rope he was carrying, and his companions were able to haul him back to shore. Days later, the men managed to paddle across, one by one, in a canoe laboriously strung together from canvas sheets and willow branches.

Early in October, Franklin ordered the company to split into three groups. George Back was to go on ahead in search of help from the Indians who lived near Fort Enterprise. Franklin would follow in his wake with the main party. Robert Hood, who was seriously ill with dysentery and swollen legs, was to remain behind. John Richardson insisted on staying with Hood in order to nurse him, and two other men also decided to stay. One of these was a *voyageur* known as Michel, a sulky character whom nobody liked.

Slipping and faltering, surviving somehow on meals of old shoes boiled in melted ice, the main group eventually managed to reach Fort Enterprise; but their joy at seeing the ramshackle hut was short-lived. The building was empty. They found out later that the Indians and the

Northwest Company clerk, having run out of provisions themselves, had left none of the replenishments they had promised. There was nothing but a note from Back, which said that he had gone on ahead to try to catch up with the Indians; if he was unable to find them, he would continue on to Fort Providence—a Northwest Company outpost that lay 150 miles away. Franklin and his group made the most of what little they had: floorboards to burn, discarded deer skins and bones to boil for soup, religious books to comfort their spirits.

On October 29 Richardson arrived with one of the men who had stayed behind. Hood and Michel were not with him. It was hours before Richardson, who was exhausted and appalled by "the ghastly countenances, dilated eyeballs and sepulchral voices of Captain Franklin and those with him," was able to bring himself to talk about what had happened back in the wilderness.

A few days before, Richardson told them, Hood and the *voyageur* Michel had been left alone, arguing over some petty matter while the other two members of the group went off to search for lichens—the only wild food now available—and firewood. A shot sounded. When he returned, Richardson discovered that Hood had been shot in the head. Michel insisted that Hood had been cleaning a gun and had killed himself accidentally, but Richardson knew the emaciated officer could barely lift a rifle, let alone clean one. Besides, the bullet had entered Hood's head from behind. Michel then armed himself with three guns, a bayonet and a knife, and took to muttering crazed remarks insinuating that he planned to repeat his crime. At his first chance, Richardson took justice

The Admiralty ship Griper, assigned to deliver explorers to the northern shore of Hudson Bay in 1824, rides out an Arctic gale. After enduring another savage storm, her dismayed captain, George Lyon, canceled the vessel's mission.

into his own hands and shot Michel. He then hastened to rejoin Franklin.

During the next week the men in the hut grew weaker, their thoughts dwelling on death. Then, on November 7, a shot outside announced reprieve. It was a party of Indians, sent by the indomitable Back to provide food. Not even Richardson, who as a doctor was aware of the consequences, could restrain himself from gorging on the meat. All were made violently sick by this unaccustomed plenty; but in a few days their bodies again grew used to a normal diet.

The ordeal was over. After a recuperative winter at Fort Providence and a 1,500-mile trek back to Hudson Bay, they arrived at their starting point on July 14, 1822. "And thus terminated," Franklin wrote, "our long, fatiguing, and disastrous travels in North America, having journeyed by water and by land (including our navigation of the Polar Sea), five thousand five hundred and fifty miles." He had illuminated what would almost certainly prove to be part of the passage, a long, central stretch of the north Canadian coast.

The mood at the Admiralty in 1824 was buoyant. With enough valiant men and rigorous effort, it was felt, the existence of a passage would soon be proved—or disproved. Without hesitation, Admiralty officials decided on four new probes. Franklin, imperturbably keen to try again, was to make another overland journey through central Canada, this time

During Franklin's reconnaissance along the Canadian coast in 1826, knife-brandishing Eskimos descend upon the expedition's boats in quest of booty. Franklin allowed the attackers to take whatever they wanted, and much of the loot was later returned. The Eskimos further rewarded the explorers' restraint by giving Franklin's men valuable information about the uncharted coast.

following the Mackenzie River to the sea, dividing his party in two, and exploring the coast to the east and west. George Francis Lyon, a 30-year-old naval commander trained in the Sahara as well as the Arctic, was to sail to Repulse Bay, then travel overland to the west in the hope of reaching Franklin's Point Turnagain. Frederick William Beechey, a surveyor and veteran of several Arctic voyages, including Parry's first, was to follow Cook's tracks through Bering Strait and probe the coast eastward beyond Icy Cape. Parry himself was to return to the age-old problem of the eastern entrance. This time he was to start at Lancaster Sound, turn south into Prince Regent Inlet and search for a way through its western side. Never before had government expenditure and confidence in a happy outcome of the quest run so high.

But once more the Arctic concealed its secrets. Locked in the ice of Baffin Bay for two months in 1824, Parry did not reach Lancaster Sound until September. By the following summer, while they were heading south through Prince Regent Inlet, his ships, the *Fury* and *Hecla* again, were driven aground by floes. The *Fury*, hopelessly damaged, stuck fast. Both crews returned to England in the *Hecla*, but not before Parry had the *Fury's* stores moved out and piled on the shore of Somerset Island. This cache of provisions, unsullied in its natural refrigeration, would save the lives of later explorers. For the present, however, Parry's voyage was a costly failure.

Beechey was scarcely more successful in the west. Penetrating Bering Strait in 1825, he anchored his ship, the *Blossom*, in Kotzebue Sound, 200 miles to the north, and sent a barge ahead to make slow and dangerous progress up the coast. Past Icy Cape, the barge—an oared craft larger and shallower than a longboat—managed to reach Point Barrow, where the land curves eastward to the mouth of the Mackenzie River. But thickening ice threatened to trap the boat on this exposed coastline, and it was forced to return to the mother vessel.

Commander Lyon had even less to report. Before his ship, the *Griper*, got even as far as Repulse Bay, she was buffeted by a devastating storm in Roes Welcome Sound. The decks were deluged with monstrous waves, while the anchors, holding off the vessel's certain destruction on a nearby reef, were strained to their limits. Lyon led his men in prayer, to prepare them for the possible death that lay only the thickness of a cable away. "Noble as the character of the British sailor is always allowed to be, in cases of danger," Lyon wrote afterward, "yet I did not believe it to be possible that among forty-one persons not one repining word should have been uttered." They soon felt that their supplications had been answered, for the storm abated. When another blew up a few days later

While exploring near the Mackenzie River, a detachment from John Franklin's expedition inscribed this hieroglyphic note at an Eskimo campsite. The pictures indicate that the explorers departed in two boats, leaving beads, a kettle and an ax as gifts for the delighted Eskimos.

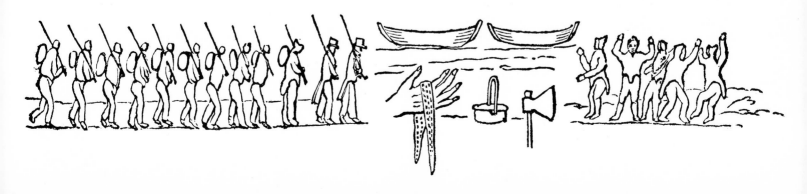

and damaged the *Griper's* hull, Lyon consulted with his officers, decided the crew had had enough, brought the ship about and returned home after five months at sea.

Amid all these melancholy tidings, only Franklin brought back new knowledge of the Northwest Passage. He reached the mouth of the Mackenzie in August 1825. The following spring, with the easiest part behind him, he sent half his men east and led the other half west, paddling along the coast in 25-foot mahogany boats. At times the sea was so shallow that the men had to get out of the boats and haul them along for miles before finding water deep enough to float their craft. All this wading through frigid waters took its toll; soon the men developed numbness and painful swellings in their legs. Nevertheless, the party charted 350 miles of coastline before Franklin decided to turn back, at a point he called Return Reef. He was only 160 miles from Point Barrow, which Captain Beechey's barge would leave 10 days later. But even if Franklin had known this and persevered in his westward plodding, he would have missed a rendezvous with Beechey. Piercing cold and barricades of ice would have stalled him for many days after Beechey abandoned Point Barrow.

In the meantime, the other half of Franklin's party had successfuly traced the coastline from the Mackenzie to the Coppermine, which brought the combined total of the expedition's achievement to 1,500 miles. Wherever the western entrance would ultimately be found, it was now apparent that the still unknown portion of the passage could barely exceed a fifth of the whole.

For the moment, the Admiralty's enthusiasm was played out. But as the decade drew to a close, a familiar figure stepped back into the Arctic drama. John Ross, having waited patiently backstage since 1818, was determined to retrieve his honor. If Parry had crushingly demonstrated his error in Lancaster Sound, he would now demonstrate that Parry had erred twice in his fruitless searches of Prince Regent Inlet in 1819 and 1824. For there, in Ross's considered judgment, was where the eastern entrance of the Northwest Passage would be found.

In acting on this conviction, he knew he could expect no assistance from an Admiralty that was dominated by John Barrow, so he turned instead to Felix Booth, a friend who had amassed a fortune in the gin-distilling business. Booth added £18,000 to the £3,000 Ross himself put up to finance the expedition.

As second-in-command, Ross chose his nephew, James Clark Ross; any strain there may have been between them was now a thing of the past. He equipped his ship, the *Victory*, with all the gadgets and instruments offered by 19th Century science, including an impressive array of compasses, chronometers, barometers, thermometers, a telescope, a theodolite and five sextants. He also had his ship fitted out with an innovation so appealing to the public's imagination that it made a visit to the *Victory* the social event of the season: the very latest high-pressure steam engine, which Ross was convinced would drive the ship through ice barriers where sails by themselves would be powerless. The *Victory* was of shallower draft and, at 150 tons, less than half the size of vessels that had been employed on recent voyages, which made her more useful

John Ross, resplendently portrayed here in a fur-draped dress uniform, was 52 years old when he emerged in 1829 from a decade of semiretirement to lead a privately financed second expedition in search of the Northwest Passage.

for inshore work. With these advantages over his rivals, Ross zestfully anticipated complete success.

He was scarcely clear of the Thames when he had cause to modify his expectations. Progress under steam was balefully slow, and the boilers leaked. Before the ship passed Land's End, on the southwestern tip of England, various pieces of "our execrable machinery" were found to be weak, worn out or badly fitted—and there were no spare parts. Off the western coast of Scotland, the boilers seized up and all but burst. To make matters worse, trouble broke out on board an accompanying vessel that had been commissioned to carry supplies to the point where the main search would begin: The crewmen of this ship decided that if they were going to proceed, it would have to be on better financial terms than those originally offered to them. Ross refused to be blackmailed and sailed on without the auxiliary.

In himself and in his men, Ross maintained a resilient morale, even when unprecedented warm weather brought out swarms of mosquitoes to plague every operation, and the temperamental steam engine demanded attention worthy of an invalid. By August 12, 1829, the stoic company of 25 had anchored off Somerset Island, where Ross saw what he had hoped to find when he gambled on leaving the auxiliary behind: the provisions left by Parry four years before, neatly stacked and in

The paddle-wheeler Victory, signal flags fluttering, receives a rousing send-off as she steams down the Thames in 1829, carrying Captain John Ross toward the Arctic. The Victory had so many breakdowns, recorded Ross, that she was "aught but a sailing ship" when she reached Canada's northern archipelago.

excellent preservation, a bounteous cornucopia waiting to be relished. The men were able to load the *Victory* with meat, bread, flour, vegetables, wines and spirits, 10 tons of coal, three boats and some valuable items of nautical equipment.

Ross now headed south into uncharted territory; paying homage to the expedition's patron, he named the land to his right Boothia Felix (it is now known as Boothia Peninsula). Along the way, he took time to describe his surroundings. "In a winter's storm the term ice conveys no idea of what it is the fate of an Arctic navigator to witness and to feel. But let them remember that ice is stone," he wrote. "Then let them imagine, if they can, these mountains of crystal hurled through a narrow strait by a rapid tide; meeting, as mountains in motion would meet, with the noise of thunder, breaking from each other's precipices huge fragments, or rending each other asunder till, losing their former equilibrium, they fall over headlong, lifting the sea around in breakers, and whirling it in eddies." Contending all the way with such conditions, the explorers made their way 130 miles beyond Parry's farthest attainment within Prince Regent Inlet. But by the end of September, every speck of sea was blanketed with an impenetrably thick layer of ice.

The *Victory's* shoal draft and her light tonnage had proved to be advantageous for maneuvering down this unmapped coastline. The engine definitely had not. Ross quickly became fed up with its erratic behavior, and as soon as he found a suitable anchorage (Felix Harbor, in Lord Mayor Bay) he ordered the engine, with all its attendant machinery, dismantled—some parts to be dumped on the shore, some to be kept and adapted to manifold uses on board the *Victory*. The Arctic baptism of steam power had been a fiasco.

In a winter marked by the usual tedium, the men busied their minds and bodies as best they could. Although they were not treated to any playhouse antics by their shipmates, they did organize hunting excursions, lectures and classes in reading, writing, mathematics and navigation. To encourage exercise, Ross required each man to take a daily walk along a sanded path he had constructed over the compressed snow that carpeted the upper deck. On Sundays all work was suspended in favor of devotions: sermons, prayers, and readings from a volume of religious tracts donated by a well-wisher back in England. But even Ross, in spite of his pluck and piety, had to acknowledge the mesmerizing boredom of winter: "Amid all its brilliancy, this land, the land of ice and snow, has ever been and ever will be a dull, dreary, heart-sinking, monotonous waste, under the influence of which the very mind is paralyzed, ceasing to care or think."

By early January 1830, the men were fending off depression with the most effective remedy of all—human companionship. When a party of 31 exuberant, tattooed Eskimos arrived to greet the strangers, the *Victory's* men welcomed them with gusto. James Clark Ross had picked up enough Eskimo language on his previous voyages to be able to smooth over introductions; and from that time on, mutual delight prevailed. Presents were exchanged, and during the days that followed there were dances, trips to the Eskimo winter camp, the usual annoyance of petty theft, the usual comic misunderstandings. The Eskimos taught the

In a fanciful illustration of the discovery of the North Magnetic Pole on June 1, 1831, James Clark Ross plants the flag on a peak near the iced-in Victory as northern lights glow overhead and three harpooners dance for joy. The pole's actual site was an abandoned Eskimo camp about 50 miles from the ship.

Englishmen frostbite prevention and demonstrated their method of hunting caribou—by disguising themselves with a caribou skin and antlers and sidling up to an unsuspecting animal for an easy kill. The Englishmen reveled in the joy of costless giving: "Let no man imagine that he knows what a present is worth," Ross wrote, "till he has found what happiness can be produced by a blue bead, a yellow button, a needle, or a piece of an old iron hoop."

In April, James Clark Ross led an overland sledge expedition to the west, taking with him two Eskimo guides and the chief mate. It was a short journey, lasting only five days, but it gave young Ross a glimpse of the sea. Ross came to the correct conclusion that the coast where the expedition had anchored was part of a peninsula extending north from the American mainland.

The Eskimos indicated that there was no channel through the peninsula; in other words, Prince Regent Inlet was the entrance to a gulf (also named Boothia) that was sealed off from the west. The expedition's chances of finding the passage were now severely reduced. The explorers would have to return to Lancaster Sound, continue westward, and drop down to the south by the next available inlet.

But as May, June and July passed, the ship remained in frozen captivity. James Clark Ross, however, escaped the tedium almost immediately; in early May he set out with the sledges and the dog teams to conduct more overland exploration. Heading west across Boothia Peninsula, he crossed to Matty Island, then explored the northern shore of a larger land mass, which John Ross later labeled King William Land on his map of the expedition's discoveries. Whether it was an island or joined Boothia Peninsula somewhere to the south was unclear. James Ross thought the two bodies were connected; but visibility was poor and rations were running short, so after building a cairn at a point he named after the *Victory*, he returned to the ship, leaving the matter unresolved.

The ice did not melt until August, and it was mid-September before the crew could begin warping, hauling and sawing their way through a three-mile barrier of pack ice separating them from the next suitable anchorage. By October their unremitting labor had advanced them scarcely 900 feet. There was no alternative but to settle in for another winter. Ross himself focused on the brighter side of their situation: their good health, their abundance of provisions, their experience in winter survival and their important discoveries so far. Realizing—as Samuel Hearne had more than 60 years earlier—that people living in a land almost devoid of vegetation could sustain their health by a diet rich in fresh oil and fats, he established generous allowances of fish and seal meat procured from the Eskimos.

In May, James Clark Ross set off on another sledge expedition, this one to locate the North Magnetic Pole. Navigators had long known that the compass needle does not point precisely to the geographic North Pole, but rather to a separate pole some distance south. Trappers and seamen approaching to within a few hundred miles of this spot found that their compasses became utterly useless: The pole pulled the compass needle downward in a way that prevented free orientation. To young Ross, the magnetic pole was more than just a nuisance; it was a scientific curiosity. By constantly observing the eccentric conduct of his own compass, he succeeded in locating the magnetic pole on the western coast of Boothia Peninsula.

Ross's delight was extravagant. "It almost seemed," he wrote, "as if our voyage and all its labors were at an end, and that nothing now remained for us but to return home and be happy for the rest of our days." Proudly erecting the British flag on the site, he took possession of the pole and its adjoining territory in the name of his country. What Ross did not know is that the magnetic pole has a chronic case of geological wanderlust; since he first pinpointed it, it has roved to the north and is now to be found some 200 miles from the point where the young explorer planted his nation's flag.

The excitement over James Ross's discovery died down as the weather turned cold once again. Compared with previous years, 1831 was calamitous. Pack ice piled up thick and fast in the Gulf of Boothia, and the *Victory* was able to force its way through no more than four miles in an entire month. The explorers resigned themselves to staying put for yet another winter. John Ross bewailed the predicament of men "weary for want of occupation, for want of variety, for want of thought." With no change in their condition, "today was as yesterday, and as was today, so would be to-morrow."

By this time Ross had become concerned about rations. He decided

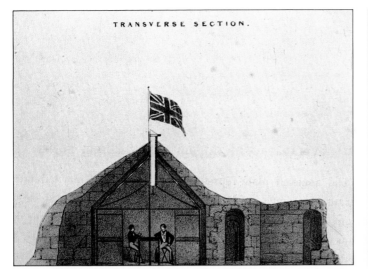

TRANSVERSE SECTION.

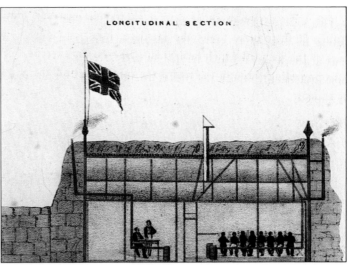

LONGITUDINAL SECTION.

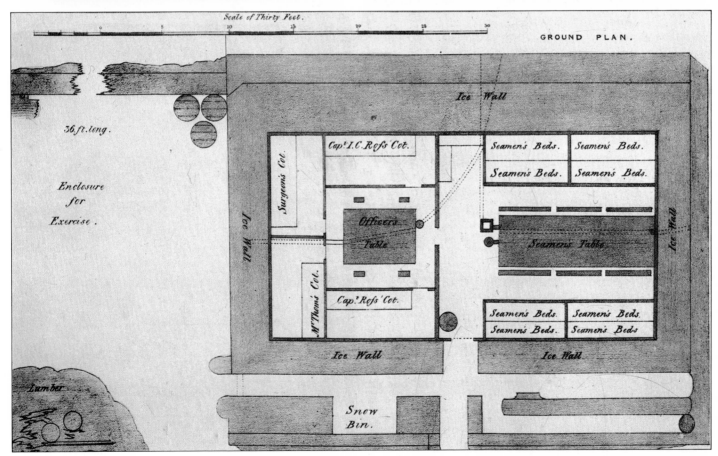

Scale of Thirty Feet.

GROUND PLAN.

This snug structure, known as Somerset House and diagramed by John Ross, housed the 21 men of his second expedition during their fourth winter in the Arctic. Built of wood and canvas, the 31-by-16-foot shelter was insulated by ice walls that were up to four feet thick.

that, in the event the ship could not be moved the following season, the men would have to track their way by foot and sledge to the beach where a portion of the stores from the *Fury* remained in place. In addition to dragging along what provisions they still had, the men would have to haul their complement of three boats the whole distance. They would then pile into these boats and take to the open sea in a desperate bid for survival.

The winter of 1831-1832 confirmed Ross's worst fears, and he reluctantly decided to abandon ship for the first time in his career. The men parted mournfully with the *Victory*, nailing her colors to the mast and drinking a last toast to "the solitary, abandoned, helpless home of our past years, fixed in immovable ice, till time should perform on her his usual work." The sick, the snow-blind and the lame trudged alongside the able-bodied, weighed down by their possessions and provisions. After five weeks, they reached Parry's legacy. The only items missing were candles, eaten by Arctic foxes.

But their ordeal was far from over. Less than two weeks later, after they had rowed 12 miles in their little craft, ice blocked the way, and the men resorted to dragging the boats again. By this means they approached Barrow Strait early in September 1832, and John Ross climbed a hill to assess their chances of escape. Barrow Strait was "an unbroken field of ice: there was not even a pool of water to be seen." By month's end, conditions had not improved, and Ross made a dismal decree: "another winter, another year," must be spent back on the beach where the *Fury's* stores lay—"if, indeed, it should be the fortune of any one to survive after another such year as the three last."

By that winter's end, scurvy had claimed the life of the ship's carpenter and had prostrated two more men. The rest of the company came through in the doubtful comfort of a makeshift, canvas-roofed dwelling they called Somerset House. By March, the luckiest, wrote Ross, were those who "dozed away their time in waking stupefaction." The crew spent April and May transporting stores to the boats, which they had left at Batty Bay, halfway to Barrow Strait. By mid-July the whole party was assembled at Batty, waiting for the ice sheet ahead to thaw.

Their luck turned on August 14. A channel appeared, enabling them to move slowly up Prince Regent Inlet. In Barrow Strait, too, the ice was breaking up. Mile by arduous mile, the boats progressed through Lancaster Sound toward Baffin Bay, where there was at least a chance that a whaler might spot them.

On August 18 they reached the bay, but a storm forced them to shelter in a harbor. A week later a sail was sighted on the horizon. The men raced toward it and were exultant when it abruptly hove to and sent a longboat out to meet them. They were delivered at last—and their salvation was as ironic as it was miraculous. Ross asked the mate in the longboat the name of his ship. It was the *Isabella*, he replied—a whaler that had once been commanded on Arctic exploration by a British naval officer named John Ross.

This was indeed the ship from whose decks Ross had mistaken a mirage for a mountain range 15 years before. Ross now identified himself. The mate expressed disbelief, insisting that Captain Ross had been dead for at least two years. No, Ross assured him, that conclusion was premature. As the boats approached the *Isabella*, her curious crew swarmed up the rigging to get a better look at this human jetsam, spat out of the Arctic and the past—"unshaven since I know not when," Ross later wrote, "dirty, dressed in the rags of wild beasts instead of the tatters of civilization, and starved to the very bones." Cheers rose from the whaling men as the castaways climbed aboard. Weeks later, after the greeting and feasting, the washing and sleeping, and the safe journey across the Atlantic, they arrived home in England to more cheers—from citizens, from peers and from King William IV himself, who received them at Windsor Castle.

Despite his record-breaking four-year sojourn in the Arctic, Ross actually had shed no new light on the Northwest Passage enigma. He had pushed on no farther than the west coast of Boothia Peninsula, expounded no new theories, charted very little new territory. But by appearing on the shores of England as if resurrected from the dead, he thrilled his countrymen in a way no earlier Arctic explorer ever had. For Ross himself, there was a greater reward than fame: By his stamina and leadership throughout the long Arctic trial, he had dispelled the shadows that had hovered about his reputation for more than a decade.

Having struggled 200 miles through Lancaster Sound to Baffin Bay in three small boats, John Ross and his men are rescued by the whaler Isabella, part of a fleet that regularly hunted in the vicinity. This engraving is based on a sketch Ross himself made of the event.

Warm record of a winter friendship

When they first meet the Eskimos, Captain John Ross and his
party abandon their weapons as they near the frightened hunters.
Ross embraced the leaders, stroking each man's clothing
in an Eskimo friendship rite. "We immediately found ourselves
established in their unhesitating confidence," he wrote.

Encounters with Eskimos provided many explorers with a welcome respite from the monotony of an Arctic winter. Such was the case for Captain John Ross and the crew of the *Victory* after ice trapped them against the southeast coast of Boothia Peninsula in 1829. By January, the Englishmen had "given up all expectations of meeting inhabitants in this place," wrote Ross. But then a group of Eskimo men appeared some distance from the ship. Ross went out to meet them, dispensed gifts, and invited them aboard for a tour.

The explorers and Eskimos soon warmed to each other. Ross's men showed off what the captain called their "marvels"—mirrors and magnifying glasses—and the visitors were properly impressed. By day's end, the two groups felt so comfortable together that they linked arms for a dance.

The Eskimos' camp was not far from the vessel, and visits back and forth continued for several months, until the Eskimos moved to a new location. Ross detailed the meetings in his journal, illustrating them in whimsical watercolors. Together, the journal and paintings form an invaluable record of Eskimo life even as they trace the developing friendship.

This old and crippled man was at the head of the first Eskimos who approached the ship. Ross later learned that he was considered the expendable member of the group and had been put in the forefront in case the Englishmen proved hostile.

Visits between unlikely neighbors

In return for their hospitable reception aboard the *Victory*, the Eskimos invited the ship's officers to their camp. There, after earning the favor of the womenfolk with gifts of glass beads and needles, the Englishmen examined the igloos, some of which were still under construction.

Ross was amazed at how quickly the people of the Arctic were able to erect their dwellings, writing that they "house themselves with a hundredth part" of the labor that the English put into their homes. But he thought the Eskimos could improve their housekeeping: Inside, garments, tools and provisions "lay about in unspeakable confusion, showing that order was not in the class of their virtues."

After that, visits occurred almost every day, gradually becoming more than social calls. The ship's surgeon journeyed to the camp to treat the ill, and the carpenter made a wooden limb for a one-legged man. An Eskimo geographer, in turn, came aboard the ship to draw Ross a detailed chart of the area; others arrived with meat or clothing to barter for trinkets. So many Eskimos poured onto the *Victory*—and left with pilfered goods—that Ross limited the number that could visit at one time. However, the benefits of the friendship outweighed its inconveniences. "Our occupations and amusements had been greater than usual," Ross wrote in midwinter, and time "passed away like a dream."

Eskimos leave their igloos to greet two of the Victory's officers. When Ross sketched the camp on his first visit, the Eskimos became uneasy. But they "were satisfied as soon as the purpose was explained, and were delighted with the identity of the representation when the sketch was finished; each recognising his own house."

Seated at a table in the Victory's cabin, an Eskimo draws a chart of the area as his wife and the ship's officers look on. When questioned about the existence of a passage to the Pacific, the Eskimos seemed confused and gave conflicting information. But they willingly provided the Englishmen with guides for several overland scouting expeditions.

Bundled in reindeer skins, an Eskimo woman sits on a bench of snow inside her igloo. Like most women of her tribe, she was short and plump and her face was covered with tattoos. Ross noted that "the females were certainly not beautiful." Still, he added, "they were, at least, not inferior to their husbands."

The emergence of a sporting rivalry

The explorers soon came to know the Eskimos well enough so that Ross referred to them by name in his journal and fondly noted their idiosyncracies (pages 124-125). But the relationship was not without its rivalries, especially in the matter of hunting and fishing. The Englishmen considered themselves accomplished sportsmen—able to teach the indigenous peoples a trick or two.

The competitiveness first surfaced in April, when Ross's nephew, James Clark Ross, and an Eskimo guide encountered a musk ox during a scouting expedition. As his dogs held the beast at bay, the Eskimo shot off several arrows, to no discernable effect. So Ross marched forward with his gun—"pleased," he wrote, "to find an opportunity of showing him the superiority of our arms." His first shots merely wounded the ox, and the enraged animal charged. But Ross coolly reloaded and—to the astonishment of his guide—felled the ox when it was only five yards away.

The Englishmen were less successful at netting fish during an outing after the ice had begun to melt. In four drags, they brought up only a few small fry and a large stone—a catch that "produced great laughter" among the Eskimos, the elder Ross recalled. The Eskimos then set off across the ice to show their skill in harpooning seals. As they closed for the kill, the quarry slipped through a crack. The Englishmen did not return the Eskimos' laughter, for, as Ross admitted, "we could not equally harpoon seals at an ice hole."

As an enraged musk ox charges, James Clark Ross steps out from behind a rock and fires, stopping the beast in its tracks. Ross recalled that when his Eskimo companion examined the musk ox a "look of horror and amazement" passed over his face as he found that one ball had shattered its shoulder and another had "passed quite through the animal."

Several Eskimos create a distraction while two harpoon-wielding hunters close in on a seal. Although the quarry managed to escape on this occasion, such demonstrations taught the Englishmen valuable techniques for capturing Arctic creatures. These skills would help them survive three more Arctic winters.

Kunana, the most successful hunter among the Eskimos, grasps a knife and the fruits of a hunting expedition. He accumulated more meat, fish and pelts than his family could use, and traded the surplus to the Englishmen for fishing hooks, metal knives and spear heads.

An Eskimo woman named Hibluna does a dance of delight upon being given a metal cutting tool, which she holds aloft along with a homemade bone knife. Ross wrote that even the most trivial present caused her to jump up and down, squealing "Owhee! Owhee!"—an exclamation that became her nickname.

An old woman called Nimna Himna attempts to sneak away from the ship with two pilfered containers. What she could not steal, she tried to obtain by guile: Once, after falling from the ship's ladder, she feigned unconsciousness and was "restored" only "by the offer of an empty tin case," wrote Ross.

Adelik, who delighted in mimicking the English, does an exaggerated imitation of an officer striding across the deck for his daily constitutional. The Eskimos could see no point in "walking up and down under the notion of exercise," reported Ross, and they took every opportunity to poke fun at the practice.

Illictu, son of the hunter Kunana (opposite page), is shown here carrying a fishhook and a rod used for probing the depth of the snow. In 1831 he provided animal skins and fuel for the journey on which James Clark Ross discovered the location of the North Magnetic Pole.

Tulluahiu, who lost a leg during an encounter with a polar bear, wears a wooden limb fashioned for him by the carpenter of the Victory. The artificial leg rendered Tulluahiu "serviceable once more to himself and his community," noted Ross, and "raised us higher in the estimation of this people than all the wonders we had shown them."

Chapter 5

"Martyrs to their country's fame"

In February 1833, eight months before John Ross and the crew of the *Victory* returned safely to England in the whaler *Isabella*, Captain George Back, whose strength and courage had sustained the journeys led by John Franklin, sailed for New York to lead an overland rescue expedition. Back planned to make his way along the Hudson's Bay Company's inland routes to Great Slave Lake, in what is now the Mackenzie District, and from there to the head of the Great Fish River, said by local Indians to flow north into the Arctic Ocean. Upon reaching the mouth of the river (later renamed after Back), the expedition was to proceed to Somerset Island in Prince Regent Inlet, on the assumption that the missing Ross would have tried to reach William Parry's old cache in the event of trouble.

The route Back was planning to take was decidedly roundabout, and even its passability was questionable, since it would take him through 800 miles of uncharted wilderness. But these were not seen as drawbacks: The expedition was prompted as much by the desire for discovery as by humanitarian impulses.

In this duality, Back foreshadowed the next quarter century of Arctic probes. Rescue efforts conjoined with the old hunger for geographical knowledge would produce unprecedented activity in the far north of the American continent, and before the latest burst of exploratory endeavor was played out, foreign specks would be scattered all across the endless icescape—cairns of piled stone, caches of food, deserted ships, monuments, flags and graves. Throughout, the Arctic held to its own unwritten timetable, yielding its secrets in an arbitrary and piecemeal fashion that compelled explorers to tempt fate again and again. John Ross had succumbed to temptation and had nearly paid with his life. Others would not be so lucky.

In April 1834, as Back was emerging from his winter quarters at the eastern end of Great Slave Lake, a messenger from the Hudson's Bay Company arrived with word of Ross's return and with modified instructions from the expedition's sponsors in England. Somerset Island was no longer on the itinerary: Back was now ordered to fill in the unmapped coastline that lay between the mouth of his river, wherever it emerged, and Franklin's Point Turnagain. He started out from Great Slave Lake in early June in high spirits. But his cheerfulness was put to the test when he tackled the river.

"River" was almost a misnomer: It was actually a series of lakes, often ice-locked, connected by narrower waters that tumbled over and around menacing rocks. The expedition's boat, weighing more than 3,000

A 19th Century cartoon offers a grim commentary on the perils of Arctic exploration. In the 1840s and 1850s, more than a dozen expeditions searched the far north for a lost contingent led by John Franklin. Of these, three required rescue missions of their own when their vessels were trapped in ice.

pounds when empty, frequently had to be portaged across hundreds of yards—sometimes miles—of rocky ground.

An added problem was the river's direction. For nearly three weeks its course was so easterly that Back feared it would debouch into Hudson Bay instead of into the Arctic Ocean as the Indians had promised. But on July 16 it at last began a distinctly northerly trend, and on July 29, "while threading our way between some sand-banks," Back later wrote, "we first caught sight of a majestic headland in the extreme distance to the north, which had a coastlike appearance." Back named the headland after the Princess Victoria and joyfully noted that, after 530 miles, the river "pours its water into the Polar Sea."

The explorers had not, in fact, reached the open ocean but had entered a long estuary that would later be named Chantrey Inlet. They pushed on through drift ice for 150 laborious miles before reaching the junction with the sea. A promontory on the west side of the estuary's mouth was given the name Point Ogle, honoring a distinguished admiral of the day. After several days' struggle with ice just beyond the point, Back accepted defeat. There was no hope of negotiating the more than 300 miles northwest to Point Turnagain by boat. Even an overland trek was ruled out, for the seasonal thaw had turned the shore into a bog that swallowed men up to their knees.

To the northeast the sea appeared to be free of ice. The expedition's second-in-command, a 22-year-old surgeon and naturalist named Richard King, recommended that they chart the coast in that direction. It was a sensible idea, but Back vetoed it. King's annoying insistence on the matter may have contributed to the captain's decision, but Back had another, more legitimate reason.

Along with the news of Ross's return, he had received maps and details of Ross's findings, including the opinion of James Clark Ross (based on his sledging expeditions) that King William Island was joined on its eastern side to Boothia Peninsula. This link was marked on Ross's map with a dotted line, a sign that he had only inferred its existence from afar. But Back chose to take the opinion for fact and believed that if he sailed northeast he would be sailing into a cul de sac. Had he been a greater explorer, he would have gone on to see for himself. As it was, he gave the order to return upriver, allowing himself to be satisfied with another man's guesswork—and in so doing, he unwittingly paved the way for tragedy 12 years later.

In June 1836, nine months after his return to England, Back was sent out again, this time in the 340-ton *Terror*, with instructions to sail to Repulse Bay, in the northwest corner of Hudson Bay. From here he was to haul boats overland, across the narrow base of Melville Peninsula (later named Rae Isthmus), and then to survey the coastline from the bottom of the Gulf of Boothia to Point Turnagain. Before the ship could reach its proposed harbor, however, it was enveloped in the thickening September pack ice and hoisted into the air "as if it were in the grasp of a giant," Back wrote.

Other explorers had been frozen into their winter quarters before, but normally only after such quarters had been carefully selected for

Thirty-six-year-old George Back was already a veteran of Arctic exploration when this portrait was sketched in 1833. From 1818 to 1837, Back took part in three expeditions, led two of his own and endured eight winters in the Arctic.

shelter—usually in the lee of cliffs, and preferably within a bay. The *Terror* was out in the open, wedged high amid an endless, rumbling chaos of ice, exposed to gales and the occasional violent disruption of the pack about her, and caught in a slow southeasterly drift that in six months carried her more than 200 miles down the northeast coast of Southampton Island.

Release did not come until midsummer of 1837, and it was accompanied by the worst travail of all. Around 9 a.m. on July 13, after teams of sailors had been working for two days to free the ship by sawing away the surrounding ice, the vessel suddenly rose and heeled over to port, "the great inclination rendering it impossible to stand on deck," Back recalled. "Then it was we beheld the strange and appalling spectacle of what may be fitly termed a submerged berg, fixed low down with one end to the ship's side, while the other, with the purchase of a long lever, advantageously placed at a right angle with the keel, was slowly rising toward the surface"—threatening to overturn the ship in the process. The end seemed inevitable. "Yet in that awful crisis there was no confusion," Back reported. The men unhooked the boats—there was no need to lower them, since they were touching water on the lee side—and filled them with clothing, arms and ammunition in readiness for the signal to abandon ship. "Happily for us," Back wrote, "there was a dead calm." He ordered the crew to attempt to separate the hull from the massive floe beneath.

The Terror, carrying George Back's final expedition, rides on her beam ends in July 1837, as crewmen frantically saw her free from ice that had fastened itself to the hull over the winter. The severely damaged ship managed to limp homeward as far as the Irish coast, where she was beached to keep her from sinking.

For 15 hours they labored with saws. By 2 o'clock the next morning the men were so exhausted that "they worked mechanically, with their eyes shut," Back remembered. Although he was anxious to have the job completed before a sudden storm or a shift in the pack ice toppled the iceberg and the ship, he ordered everyone to "quit the ice and lie down for two hours." Then, as he contemplated his crewmen "stretched out in death-like slumber on the lee side," he was startled by the grating noise of ice breaking up. "Before a word could be spoken," Back reported, "the liberated ship righted entirely; while broken spars, the bent saw, and the massy berg, were all in commotion together." The pack ice had shifted, but instead of capsizing the *Terror*, it had released her into her rightful element once again.

There was no question of trying to resume their mission. Neither the ship—"crazy, broken, and leaky"—nor the scurvy-weakened crew was in any condition for further Arctic duty: As it was, the *Terror* barely kept her nose above water on the journey home. The voyage marked the end of Back's exploring career. His health had suffered irreparable damage during successive ordeals in the north, and he now retired to a knighthood and several lesser distinctions, leaving the unexplored section of the Arctic coastline to be charted by others.

Richard King was more than willing to step in. During the time Back was away on the *Terror*, his erstwhile companion—in an effort to boost his own Arctic aspirations—had written a singularly snide version of the journey they had shared down the Great Fish, or Back, River. King not only took every opportunity to denigrate his former captain—he, King, would succeed, he said, where "a Parry, a Franklin and a Back" had failed—but he also spoke ill of the Hudson's Bay Company. By his arrogance and indiscretion he managed to alienate everyone whose assistance he would find necessary for any voyage of discovery. His petitions to lead a return expedition to the Back River were met with icy silence by the offended Arctic Establishment, and King faded into obscurity for the next decade.

In the meantime, two employees of the Hudson's Bay Company, working together, were quietly performing prodigies of exploration in the Arctic. One was an irascible young Scot named Thomas Simpson, a former seminary student whose cousin, George Simpson, headed the company. The other was Peter Warren Dease, the company's chief factor. Dease was nominally Simpson's superior, but the younger man's energy dictated the pace and the scope of their accomplishment.

Simpson and Dease spent three successive exploring seasons mapping the northern shores of the American continent. In the summer of 1837 they descended the Mackenzie River and headed west along the coast by boat. Beyond Return Reef—Franklin's farthest attainment in 1826—ice prevented any more progress in the boats. But Simpson and a small party continued westward on foot and by Eskimo canoe, covering the remaining territory to Point Barrow, which had been reached from the Pacific by Captain Frederick Beechey in 1825. The coastline was thus charted from Bering Strait, through Return Reef, to Franklin's Point Turnagain—1,150 miles in all.

The following summer Simpson and Dease returned to the Arctic in

A web of routes to final victory

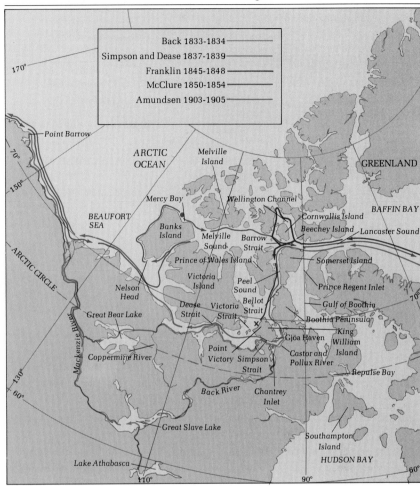

Filling in gaps on the Arctic map, George Back traveled by river to Chantrey Inlet, and Thomas Simpson and Peter Dease charted the northern coastlines of Alaska and Canada from Point Barrow east. Sir John Franklin's ships cleared Peel Sound but were abandoned near King William Island. Searching for Franklin, Robert McClure's expedition was trapped off Banks Island, then rescued and transported home via Baffin Bay. In 1905, Roald Amundsen completed the Northwest Passage, traveling east to west.

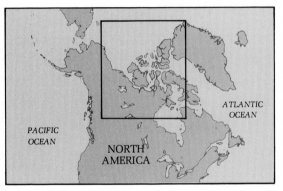

boats, hoping to settle the outline of the coast between Point Turnagain and Chantrey Inlet, the estuary of the Back River. After battling persistent coastal ice from the mouth of the Coppermine River east to within three miles of Point Turnagain, their boats were halted (the explorers euphemistically named the spot Boathaven). Leaving Dease behind, Simpson and a few men set off on foot with 10 days' provisions. Although the shore was swampy and the going painfully slow, Simpson managed to advance about 100 miles beyond Boathaven, reaching the eastern end of the channel later known as Dease Strait. Ahead, the sea was open, holding out the promise of eventual success. But two of his men were lame, so Simpson reluctantly retreated.

The next season in the Arctic brought additional progress. A milder winter and warmer summer created a wide channel between the shore and the pack ice beyond Boathaven, and the expedition reached the eastern end of Dease Strait on July 26, 1839, nearly a month earlier than in the previous year. They then found and penetrated Simpson Strait, south of King William Island, and in mid-August arrived at Chantrey Inlet, where they came upon a cache of pemmican left under a cairn five years earlier by Back. They had completed their assignment: The coastline was now mapped from Bering Strait to Chantrey Inlet. "But Mr. Dease and myself were not quite satisfied," Simpson wrote—though it is more likely that he spoke mainly for himself. At any rate, Dease agreed to do what Back had once decided against: to push farther east.

Simpson wanted to determine whether Boothia Peninsula was connected to the mainland. After covering nearly 70 miles of the coast in the face of a bitter northeast wind, the explorers were forced to seek shelter on August 20 in the mouth of a small river, which they named Castor and Pollux after their boats. Overhead, flocks of Canada geese were streaming south, a noisy signal of the approaching winter. "It was now quite evident to us," Simpson wrote, "that the time was come for commencing our return to the distant Coppermine River, and that any further foolhardy perseverance could only lead to the loss of the whole party." Before leaving, Simpson climbed a ridge to make a survey. Although his account is not very clear, he evidently thought that they had reached a point east of Boothia, and that the isthmus connecting it to the mainland did not exist. He concluded that it was possible to sail from the mouth of the Back River into the Gulf of Boothia. But proof would have to wait until he could return the next year.

The explorers now retraced their route, deviating enough to investigate about 60 miles of the south shore of King William Island (which Simpson believed was connected to Boothia) and some 150 miles of the south shore of Victoria Island (named by him the year before). On September 16 they were back at the Coppermine River, having traversed more than 1,600 miles of polar sea in open boats—the longest such voyage so far attempted in one season.

If Simpson had come back, as he intended, he probably would have cleared up his geographical errors. But in mid-June, while he was en route to New York and thence to London (he was concerned at not having received permission for the next expedition), he died under mysterious circumstances. One of the four men who were with him as they crossed the Minnesota prairie testified that Simpson—who had already shown signs of extreme nervous tension—had imagined that his companions were conspiring to kill him. He shot two of them; the others escaped, then returned the next morning with reinforcements. Whether these men shot Simpson or discovered that he had already taken his own life is not known.

Thomas Simpson died just shy of his 32nd birthday. He had completed the coastal survey begun by Beechey and Franklin, establishing the existence of a sea-lane that overlapped by 20° of longitude the lane that had been exposed by Parry's record-shattering drive through Lancaster Sound to Melville Island. The problem was that these two navigable tracks ran roughly parallel to each other, separated by some 900 miles of unknown sea and land. Moreover, each of them appeared to have been taken to the limit: Parry's path had been blocked by apparently permanent ice, Simpson's by the land of Boothia Isthmus (for he was virtually alone in his misconception that Boothia was an island). The next logical step was to search for a north-south link, somewhere west of Boothia and east of Melville Island.

CAPTAIN SIR JOHN FRANKLIN

A bemedaled Sir John Franklin and three of his officers sit for daguerreotype portraits shortly before they embarked from England in May 1845 to investigate waters that were expected to be the final link in the Northwest Passage.

CAPTAIN FRANCIS CROZIER

COMMANDER JAMES FITZJAMES

ICE MASTER JAMES REID

The Admiralty turned to that task in 1844. There was no difficulty in assigning ships for the voyage. The 340-ton *Terror* had already shown her resilience, not only during Back's ice-buffeted ordeal in 1837, but in a subsequent four-year spell of Antarctic exploration under James Clark Ross. And a sister-ship, the 370-ton *Erebus*—in Greek mythology, the passageway to Hades—had likewise survived Antarctic rigors, being once driven broadside against an iceberg while maneuvering through an ice field. Both ships were additionally outfitted with steam engines and screw propellers far more reliable than the primitive propulsion system that had vexed John Ross in the *Victory*.

The appointment of a commander was a more complicated question. Worthy veterans of Arctic service were not lacking, but obstacles nullified the candidacies of several of them. At 44, James Clark Ross had commanded more polar voyages than any man alive and was as highly regarded by the Admiralty as by the men who had served under him. But in 1843 Ross had married, agreeing to a condition imposed by his wife's parents that he voyage no more. Of the other names in the Arctic galaxy, Parry was 54 and long since retired from active seamanship. Sir John Ross was approaching 70 and, with his old enemy Barrow serving out his last year as Secretary of the Admiralty, unlikely to be seriously considered. Barrow's own favorite candidate was a talented and popular naval officer named James Fitzjames, but the Lords of the Admiralty barred Fitzjames from command on the grounds that he was too young—although at 33 he was older than Parry had been at the time of his finest achievement.

Sir John Franklin, recently returned from a tour as Governor of Tasmania, was itching to take another crack at the Arctic and, unlike James Ross, had a wife who would not try to dissuade him. When the First Lord of the Admiralty replied to Franklin's spirited application that he was 60 years of age, Sir John protested, "No, no, my lord, only 59." Parry supported Franklin's claim, telling the First Lord, "He is a fitter man to go than any I know, and if you don't let him go, the man will die of disapointment." Franklin's virtues—stamina, tenacity and his undoubted powers of command—all argued for him, and the Admiralty finally granted him the appointment.

On May 19, 1845, the two ships sailed from England, Franklin on the *Erebus*, with Fitzjames as his second, and Captain Francis Crozier, another Arctic veteran, in command of the *Terror*. The two vessels were stocked with "every species of provisions for three years," according to the captain of the tender that accompanied them across the Atlantic, carrying additional supplies. "They had also stores of every description for the same time, and fuel in abundance."

The instructions Franklin received from the Admiralty left him a good deal of discretion. He was directed to proceed west through Lancaster Sound for about 350 miles, until, on the port side, he sighted Cape Walker, a headland that had been noted by Parry in 1819. Since Parry had indicated an impenetrable wall of ice some distance to the west of this, Franklin was ordered to follow any seaway leading to the south, in order to reach the coast of the mainland. If this proved impossible, he was to look to the north.

One thing the Admiralty had not provided was a scheme for rescuing the expedition if something should go wrong. The sensible procedure would have been to agree to dispatch a vessel to a rendezvous at Cape Walker if no news from Franklin had been received after two years. But Franklin and his supporters were afraid that the government would refuse to send an expedition at all if the possibility of failure was even considered.

Still, the auspices for success were good, and among the ships' officers and men morale was high on the journey to Arctic waters. Ice master James Reid, who was responsible for assessing the thickness and condition of ice lying ahead of the bows, reassured Fitzjames on the matter of icebergs: "Let it come on to blow," Reid said, "look out for a big un. Get under his lee, and hold to him fast, sir. If he drifts to land, why, he grounds afore you do." Fitzjames wrote down the ice master's advice, along with his own opinions of the "delightful" Franklin and the crew—"fine hearty fellows, mostly north-country men." He also recorded details of the fog and gales they encountered, and of their first glimpse of the ominous, noiseless iceblink—the white glare reflected on the sky by vast sheets of ice.

On July 6, Fitzjames sent his impressions back to England by way of the tender from a Danish settlement on Disko Island, off the western coast of Greenland. On July 12, Franklin's two vessels set sail from Disko, worked their way up the coast of Greenland for 350 miles, then struck out across Baffin Bay. On July 26 they were spotted by an Aberdeen whaler, which reported them moored to an iceberg roughly in the latitude of Lancaster Sound. Years would pass before Europe would see or hear anything of the expedition again.

Though many details will remain forever in dispute, the route the two ships took can be discerned from remains that came to light afterward and from Eskimo reports of the tragic last act of the Franklin drama. In their first season the ships cleared Lancaster Sound and penetrated Barrow Strait, probably as far as Cape Walker. Here the pack ice prevented further progress westward or southward. Franklin fell back on his secondary plan, trying a northward bypass of Melville Island—where Parry had been balked—by sailing up Wellington Channel. Ice stopped him north of Cornwallis Island, but he did succeed in sailing around the island and returning to Beechey Island, at the junction of Barrow Strait and Wellington Channel. There he halted for the first winter, and there three men died and were buried.

The summer of 1846 was an extremely mild one. But its mildness was only bait held out by malevolent fate. The ships tried to go south again, and this time they succeeded, discovering and getting through a sound between Prince of Wales and Somerset Islands. The channel was later named after Sir Robert Peel, the Prime Minister who had given final approval for the Franklin expedition. As the explorers emerged from Peel Sound, success must have seemed close. They were halfway to the continental coastline already explored by Simpson, and from that stretch of shore the whole of the route to Bering Strait had already been tracked. But then their luck began to ebb. They met an unrelenting blanket of ice on the northwestern side of King William Island, in what

H.M.S. "Erebus": a warship adapted to battle the Arctic

When Sir John Franklin and his men set forth to find the Northwest Passage in 1845, their hopes of winning through to glory were founded at least in part on the quality of their two ships, the *Erebus* and *Terror*—a matching pair represented by the *Erebus* here and on the following pages.

Like many other Arctic discovery ships in the 19th Century, the 370-ton *Erebus* had begun her life as a bomb vessel, a Royal Navy warship designed to carry shell-firing mortars. In order to bear the weight of two of the three-ton weapons and to withstand their tremendous recoil, the ship was given an unusually sturdy shape. With a hull 105 feet long and a 29-foot beam, she resembled a shoe box: Her bow was bluff, her bottom was flat, and her stern rose steeply from her keel. This squared-off design did not aid her speed—her maximum was only about eight knots, and she usually lumbered along at less than half that rate—but it

did provide her with a roomy hold, well-suited for carrying supplies for Franklin's crew.

For all her native strength, the *Erebus* was reinforced with additional planking before her voyage to the Arctic, where mammoth ice floes could crush a ship like an empty nutshell. Her bow, wrote a London reporter, was built up into "a mass of timber about eight feet thick," and it was covered with plates of sheet iron, enabling the *Erebus* to butt her way through pack ice.

Even the *Erebus'* rig was adapted for her Arctic mission. As a bomb vessel, she had set square sails from all three of her masts; but for her new role, the mizzenmast was re-rigged to carry fore-and-aft sails. The advantage of this rig was its simplicity: It could be handled by fewer men—and fewer would be along on the expedition because so much of the ship's interior space had to be devoted to stores.

H.M.S. EREBUS

To increase the *Erebus'* ability to cope with Arctic storms, fickle winds and shifting ice, the Navy outfitted her with a remarkable auxiliary power plant. They purchased a 25-horsepower locomotive from the London & Greenwich Railway, removed its front wheels and lowered the 15-ton engine crosswise into the *Erebus'* hold. They then extended a shaft 32 feet from the locomotive's driving wheel to the ship's stern, where they attached a seven-foot propeller.

The propeller itself was the focus of considerable ingenuity. If ice threatened to damage it, crewmen were to remove the iron storage tank above the propeller opening, then hoist the propeller on deck through a vertical well. To prevent the formation of ice in the vacated space, they would plug the gap with large wooden chocks, then put the storage tank back in place.

Another ingenious feature was a desalinator built into the galley stove: To augment the ship's water supply, the device removed salt from sea water even as it was being used to steam food. Directly below was a huge boiler. It warmed the ship by sending hot water through a network of pipes.

Although the locomotive took up a great deal of room in the hold, the *Erebus* managed to carry provisions sufficient to last three years. The stores included 35 tons of flour, 24 tons of meat, 1,896 gallons of liquor, 1¾ tons of tobacco, nearly a ton of soap and more than half a ton of candles—plus a barrel organ, a primitive camera for taking daguerreotypes, and all the scientific instruments needed to study Arctic magnetism, geology, botany and zoology.

With their ship crammed full of food and equipment, the *Erebus'* 67-man crew was berthed in whatever crannies remained. While Commander Fitzjames, the ship's second-in-command, enjoyed comparative luxury in a cabin six feet wide, the common seamen slung their hammocks side by side on the mess deck.

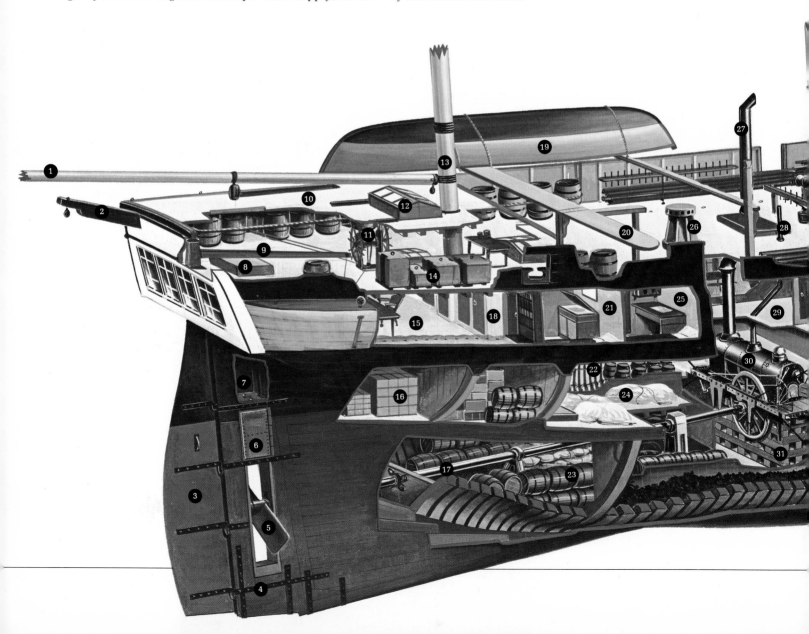

1. DRIVER BOOM
2. DAVIT
3. RUDDER
4. IRON REINFORCING STRAPS
5. PROPELLER
6. IRON STORAGE TANK
7. PROPELLER WELL
8. HATCH FOR ACCESS TO WELL
9. TILLER
10. POOP DECK
11. STEERING WHEEL
12. SKYLIGHT
13. MIZZENMAST
14. CHOCKS FOR PROPELLER OPENING
15. CAPTAIN'S CABIN
16. STOWAGE
17. PROPELLER SHAFT
18. LOCKERS
19. SHIP'S BOAT

20. BRIDGE
21. CAPTAIN'S BED CABIN
22. ARMS STAND
23. STOWAGE
24. SAIL ROOM
25. FIRST LIEUTENANT'S CABIN
26. CAPSTAN
27. EXHAUST FUNNEL
28. STEAMPIPE
29. LOWER DECK
30. LOCOMOTIVE ENGINE
31. ENGINE SUPPORTS
32. FRAMES
33. COAL
34. PURSER'S CABIN
35. PUMPS
36. MAINMAST
37. MAIN HATCH
38. EXTRA PLANKING

39. PROJECTION TO SHIELD RIGGING
40. DEADEYES
41. ILLUMINATORS
42. SPARE SPARS
43. FORE HATCH
44. STOVE FUNNEL
45. GALLEY STOVE
46. HOT WATER BOILER
47. IRON WATER TANKS
48. STOWAGE
49. WINDLASS
50. FOREMAST
51. FORWARD PART OF MESS DECK
52. UPPER DECK
53. SICK BAY
54. REINFORCED BOW
55. IRON SHEATHING
56. CATHEAD
57. BOWSPRIT

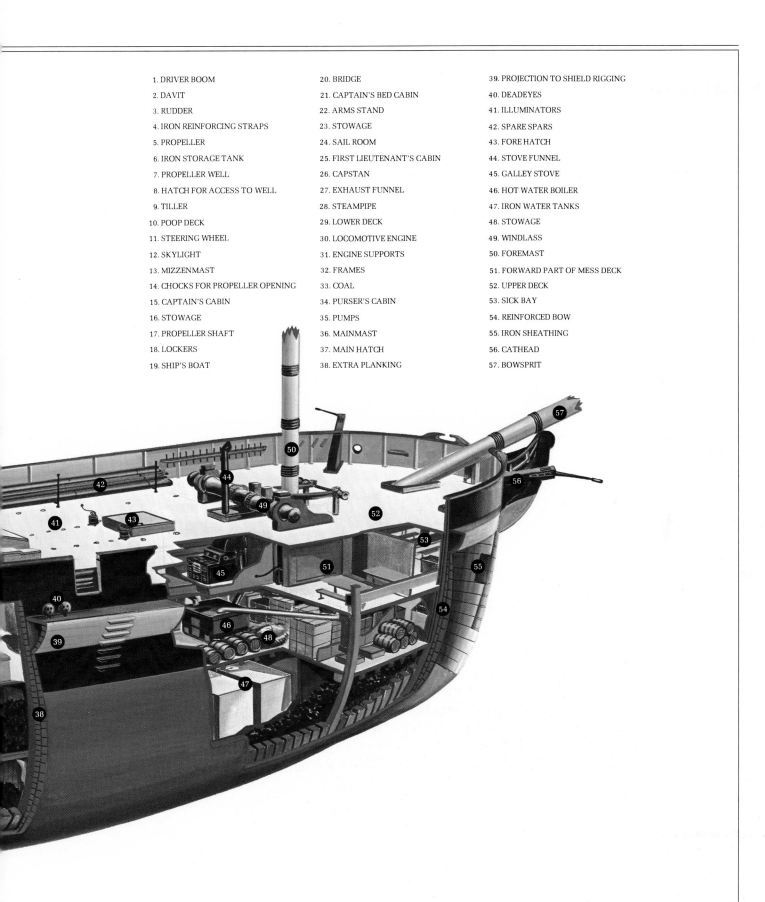

would later be named Victoria Strait, and by September were locked in for their second winter.

Franklin was up against a permanent barrier: The massive pack that blocked him was constantly reinforced by the winds and currents that sweep off the Beaufort Sea, through Melville Sound and around the northeast corner of Victoria Island into what was later named McClintock Channel. While the 1846 season still left him the option, he could have tried the one alternative path to the south: He might have gone around to the narrower channel east of King William Island—a channel sheltered by the island from the worst assaults of the south-drifting pack—and settled for the winter near Chantrey Inlet. In the following season he could have moved on to crowning glory. But Franklin did not take this course because he did not believe it existed. His charts, based on the erroneous conclusion first reached by James Clark Ross and compounded by Back and Simpson, told him that King William Island was joined by an isthmus to Boothia. No purpose could be served by sailing down the island's east coast, so Franklin kept to the west, and the *Terror* and the *Erebus* were trapped in ice from which no human agency would ever release them.

The winter of 1846 must have been a dreadful ordeal. The two vessels

Several of Britain's most illustrious explorers appear in this portrayal of the Arctic Council, a group formed to advise the Admiralty in its efforts to locate the missing Franklin expedition. Sir John Richardson indicates a point on a chart for the seated Sir Francis Beaufort, chief hydrographer of the Royal Navy, while Sir George Back confers at left with white-haired Sir William Parry. Sir James Clark Ross stands between Beaufort and a portrait of John Franklin.

were caught some 15 miles from shore, piteously exposed to the gales that swept from the northwest across hundreds of unobstructed miles. Hunting parties that made the arduous trek to King William Island would have found little reward for their labor, for the island was almost devoid of wildlife. Still, Franklin and his men probably kept up their spirits with the thought that the ships would break through Victoria Strait after the spring thaw.

There was no thaw. During 1847 the ice remained solid, as the ice in this quarter almost always does, and the ships stayed where they were. In June, Franklin died, at the age of 61. By the following spring a total of nine officers and 15 crewmen were dead. Provisions were nearly exhausted. During April and May of 1848, the survivors, now reduced to 105, abandoned their ships and slowly trudged south, apparently hoping to make their escape overland along the Back River. They were diseased and famished. Some gave up and turned back toward the ships. Some died in their tracks. The strongest trekked on, down King William Island and across Simpson Strait to the continental coast west of Point Ogle. Sledges with invalids on them were abandoned along the way. Once on the mainland, even the strongest had no strength left. In their last extremities some fed on the bodies of their dead comrades. It would have been small consolation to the dying men to know that in reaching Simpson Strait they had forged a final link in the chain of connection from east to west.

Despite the lack of news from Franklin during 1846, official England felt no immediate concern. Not only did the expedition have provisions for three years, but careful rationing augmented by hunting could probably stretch the supplies to last a year or two beyond that. But as 1847 wore on, the continuing silence bespoke a serious hitch in Franklin's plans, and anxiety in England began to mount. After due consultation with Arctic veterans such as James Clark Ross, Beechey, Parry and Back, the Admiralty decided to send out three separate rescue expeditions to make a thorough search of Franklin's intended route. In the interests of covering all possibilities, Beechey urged that a fourth group be sent down the Back River to look near King William Island and Boothia. Dr. Richard King also proposed such an expedition, with himself in charge. But James Ross was utterly convinced that the missing ships had been caught in ice somewhere west of Cape Walker, and both Beechey and King were overruled.

The rescuers left in 1848. One ship, the *Plover*, sailed in January by way of Cape Horn to watch for Franklin's emergence to the north of Bering Strait; there she would be joined by the *Herald*, redeployed from a surveying assignment off the coast of California. Two other ships, the *Enterprise* and the *Investigator*, commanded by James Clark Ross, left in June to track Franklin through Lancaster Sound to and beyond Cape Walker. (Ross's wife, in response to a plea from Lady Franklin, had released him from his wedding promise not to go to sea again.) And an overland expedition was sent by way of the Mackenzie River to hunt along the Arctic coastline.

None of the expeditions found any trace of Franklin or his ships, but

The indomitable Lady Jane Franklin, seen as a young woman in this 1816 portrait, personally sponsored four Arctic expeditions between 1850 and 1857 to seek evidence of her husband's fate.

Ross came closest. His effort was also notable in that it gave two promising young officers—Robert McClure and Leopold McClintock, serving as Ross's first and second lieutenants on the *Enterprise*—invaluable experience in Arctic exploration, thus preparing them for their own ambitious expeditions.

Ross spent the bitter winter of 1848-1849 on the northeast corner of Somerset Island, at Port Leopold (named by him after Queen Victoria's uncle, the first King of the Belgians). In the spring, several sledge parties went out to reconnoiter. Ross and McClintock traveled 150 miles down the frozen waste of Peel Sound before turning back; the ice covering the sound seemed impenetrable, and it never occurred to Ross that, in the freakishly warm summer of 1846, Franklin's ships could have sailed through the channel without obstruction. Meanwhile, another sledge party traveled south, while a third headed north, across Barrow Strait. Unfortunately, the third party did not reach Beechey Island, site of Franklin's first winter camp.

In November 1849, Ross returned home, where he was subjected to severe criticism for his poor showing. England was by now seriously alarmed about Franklin's disappearance, and the public wanted action. Old Sir John Ross, citing a compact he had made with Franklin in 1845 to conduct a rescue mission if needed, pressed his claim to the Admiralty, which denied it. Richard King was besieging various authorities with offensive memorandums insisting that he was the best qualified person to lead a rescue expedition. It should go down the Back River, he said, and press the search between King William and Victoria Islands. His theory of where to look was—quite inexplicably—correct. But the Admiralty coolly declined King's assistance in the matter.

Instead, it mounted new searches from both east and west. Captain Horatio Austin, who had been Parry's first lieutenant in 1824, was given command of a four-ship flotilla consisting of the cargo vessels *Resolute* and *Assistance* and the steamers *Pioneer* and *Intrepid*. Austin was instructed to search Wellington Channel and Melville Island. Under separate orders in the eastern division were two brigs—the *Lady Franklin* and the *Sophia* (named after Sophia Cracroft, Lady Franklin's devoted friend and companion through these trials)—commanded by William Penny, an Aberdeen whaling captain with considerable experience in the Arctic. For the western approach, the *Enterprise* and the *Investigator*, only recently returned from James Ross's unproductive expedition, were refitted, given new crews and sent out again, this time to enter through Bering Strait.

Private enterprise got into the act as well, for the cause had gained worldwide attention. Thwarted in his petition to the Admiralty, Sir John Ross fitted out the 120-ton *Felix* for Arctic work by taking public subscriptions, while Lady Franklin dispatched Captain Charles C. Forsyth in the schooner *Prince Albert*. Determined to pursue all possible sources of help, Lady Franklin had also written to President Zachary Taylor to plead for American assistance in the search. Taylor was receptive, as was Congress, which defrayed a portion of the expense of outfitting the brigs *Advance* and *Rescue* (the rest was borne by the New York merchant Henry Grinnell).

Robert McClure, seen here in Arctic hunting clothing, ignored orders in 1850 when he sailed without escort 1,000 miles eastward from Bering Strait in the search for Franklin—and in hopes of finding the Northwest Passage himself. His act cost him dearly: Ice held him fast for three winters near Banks Island.

Thus, in 1850, no fewer than 12 exploratory ships were directed to disturb the cold isolation of the far north. This surge of activity was by no means free of self-interest. The Admiralty had offered a reward of £20,000 to any expedition that located Franklin or his crews. And, inevitably, there were some commanders who were keener to find the Northwest Passage themselves than to rescue an explorer who had failed (Sir John Ross suspected that his nephew had been guilty of this ambition on the voyage from which he had just returned). Still others, doubtful that a passage would ever be effected, concentrated on exploration of the large expanse of the Arctic archipelago that remained blank on the map, the only prize being an obscure immortality in giving their names to remote capes and peaks.

Lady Franklin was alone in having a clear and uncomplicated motive: She wanted to confirm her belief that her husband, whether or not he returned, had actually filled in the final gap in the passage. Her efforts to solve the mystery of his disappearance would continue for the best part of a decade, and would result in the most thorough charting of the still-unknown parts of the region.

Because they had the farthest to go, the first ships to depart in 1850 were the *Enterprise* and the *Investigator*, which left London on January 10. In command was Captain Richard Collinson, who sailed aboard the *Enterprise*. James Clark Ross's former lieutenant, Robert McClure, was captain of the *Investigator*. Since the *Enterprise* was the faster vessel, she took the lead on the journey round Cape Horn and up through the Pacific. Collinson had given instructions that the two ships should rendezvous off the coast of Alaska. When the *Investigator* reached Honolulu on July 1, McClure learned that Collinson had left only 24 hours earlier. From another seaman he also learned of another route to the northern coast of Alaska, a shortcut that would take him through a narrow gap in the long barrier of land and reefs that make up the Aleutian Islands. By following this course he arrived at the Cape Lisburne rendezvous in late July, several weeks in advance of Collinson.

McClure was an ambitious, stern and moody man, and he was acutely conscious that commanding the first ship through the Northwest Passage would be quite as noteworthy an achievement as discovering the fate of Franklin. It seemed to him that the chance of an early accomplishment of either mission would be impaired by waiting for the *Enterprise* to catch up. Disregarding the advice of Captain Henry Kellett of the *Herald*, who had been stationed in Bering Strait ever since 1848, McClure elected to push on. His decision could be justified on the grounds of the urgency of his mission, but it was always to seem tainted by an excessive desire for personal glory.

The *Investigator* struggled eastward along the northern Canadian coast, sometimes halted by head winds, but eventually passing the mouth of the Mackenzie River, then Cape Bathurst and Cape Parry. From time to time Eskimos were encountered. Although the company included an interpreter—an amiable German missionary named Johann Miertsching—nothing could be learned of Franklin. Just beyond Cape Parry, ice forced McClure to move away from the coast and into unexplored waters. It was now early September, and the temperature was

dropping rapidly, but the ship managed to follow a zigzag path through the floes. On September 6 land was sighted—a looming height on the southern shore of Banks Island. McClure named it Nelson Head. A few days later the *Investigator* came into Prince of Wales Sound, which separates Banks Island from Victoria Island and gives access at its other end to Melville Sound.

On September 11 the ship was caught in a pack and for nearly a week was driven northward with the pack, coming to within 50 miles of Melville Sound before the wind drove both ice and ship back. On the night of the 25th, as the *Investigator* neared a pair of small midchannel islands that McClure had named the Princess Royal Islands, a prodigious storm struck. "For 17 hours," remembered the missionary Miertsching, "we stood ready on deck where each moment appeared to be our last; great massive pieces of ice three and four times the size of the ship were pushed one on top of another and under continuing pressure forced into a towering heap, which would then come tumbling down with a thunderous roar." The crew broke into the spirit store and drank themselves numb. "Then spoke the mercy of God," Miertsching wrote. " 'Thus far shalt thou go, but no farther;' the commotion in the ice died away, and it lay without the least motion."

October brought calm weather and lacerating cold. The *Investigator* was now firmly locked in the frozen channel, and McClure and his men prepared themselves for the dark months ahead. If nothing else, the captain could take satisfaction in knowing that he was well positioned to do some productive exploring by sledge in the spring.

While McClure was going his headstrong way in the west, the eastern flotilla—Austin's four naval vessels, Penny's two brigs, John Ross's *Felix* and Lady Franklin's *Prince Albert*—entered Lancaster Sound. The two American ships joined them for a time, but they had not been adequately provisioned to winter over and left the search party in mid-September. As it happened, the Americans were caught shortly afterward by the ice and trapped for nearly nine months, suffering terribly from cold and scurvy. The *Prince Albert* was luckier. After making a reconnaissance of Prince Regent Inlet until blocked by ice, Captain Forsyth met up briefly with some of the fleet in Barrow Strait and then returned to England, arriving on October 1.

Forsyth brought home the first news of the lost explorers, for in late August the location of Franklin's winter quarters on Beechey Island had been discovered. All that remained were graves bearing the names

Lifted and tilted by clashing polar ice, McClure's Investigator winters in Prince of Wales Strait, the channel he thought would give him access to Melville Sound and thence the Atlantic. Arguing "the absolute importance of retaining every mile," he had refused to retreat to a safer anchorage—thus subjecting the ship to the full force of winter gales.

of two men of the *Erebus* and one of the *Terror*, dated January and April 1846, along with a few items of equipment and other traces of occupation. Exhaustive searching revealed no hint of where Franklin had intended to go from there.

The seven other ships of the flotilla, well provisioned for winter, settled into icy berths in and about the entrance to Wellington Channel. The men walked from one ship to another without difficulty. John Ross—whose last Arctic winter, in 1833, had been considerably less pleasant—wrote that he found Captain Penny, who was berthed nearby on the *Lady Franklin,* "an excellent and kind neighbour; he had luxuries which I could not afford, and was liberal in sharing them with me." And although the four crews under Austin might not have had many luxuries, their commander was zealous in looking after their health and maintaining morale. Taking a leaf from Parry's book, Austin instituted shipboard dramatics and lectures of various sorts. Some of the men occupied themselves with making sculptures in the snow, others with hunting fox and polar bear—although the latter was canny game, and only one was taken during that winter.

Leopold McClintock, now assigned to the *Assistance,* spent the winter working out methods of extending the range of overland explorers. He designed sledges that were lighter than any used before and prepared for long spring journeys by making shorter trips to plant advance food depots, protected and identified by conspicious stone cairns. McClintock also devised tactics involving support crews. One or two crews would travel with the main company, carrying the provisions for the first part of the journey; the support crew would then turn back, leaving the main group to proceed with its own supplies intact. Later, the support team might be sent out again to plant caches against the main party's return. And McClintock conceived a scheme to conserve energy when deep bays had to be searched: Two sledge parties would split up, one taking a shortcut across the mouth of the bay with a heavy sledge carrying the bulk of the provisions, while the other traced the coastline with a lighter load.

A flotilla of rescue vessels assembles off Beechey Island in 1850 after traces of Franklin's 1845-1846 camp were found there. The large ships at left and right are Captain Horatio Austin's barks Resolute and Assistance, under tow by their steam-powered consorts Intrepid and Pioneer.

The sledge crews prepared themselves throughout March, and on April 4, 1851, more than 200 men lined up in long columns at the northwest corner of Griffith Island, near Cornwallis Island, ready and eager to go. After listening to a rousing speech from Austin, they started out in two large divisions, one to the south, the other to the west. The men traveled at night and slept during the daytime, when marginally warmer temperatures made it safer to stop moving. They marched for eight to 10 hours at a stretch, taking only a brief pause for a meal of frozen pork fat, a biscuit and some rum. When the wind was right and the surface of the ice was not too hummocky, sails were set on the sledges to speed their progress.

The results were spectacular. Wellington Channel was thoroughly surveyed, as was the west coast of Prince of Wales Island and part of the east coast of Victoria Island. One sledge party traveled down Peel Sound, fighting a blizzard almost the entire way, and came to the conclusion that ice probably filled the channel to its floor, barring it perpetually to shipping. The most notable journey was led by McClintock himself, who went westward to Melville Island, left a record of his ship's position on top of Parry's Monument and then returned to the *Assistance*, covering a total of 770 miles in 80 days. All told, the sledge parties traveled more than 7,000 miles.

But no additional evidence of the Franklin expedition was found, except some suspect fragments of English elm floating in a channel just

The silhouetted tombstones of three of Franklin's men—a seaman, a stoker and a Royal Marine—stand like melancholy guards under the midnight sun of Beechey Island. This engraving was based on a sketch made by American surgeon-explorer Elisha Kent Kane in 1850.

north of Cornwallis Island. Austin and his fellow commanders returned to England in the fall of 1851 with nothing more to show for their labors than the knowledge of where Franklin had spent his first winter—and even that, thanks to the early return of the *Prince Albert,* was old news. Neither the Admiralty nor the public was much impressed, although more than 20 veterans of the exercise wrote memoirs, mostly inflated, of their experiences.

In April 1852 the Lords of the Admiralty—paying more attention to public opinion than to their own judgment—dispatched another fleet to continue the search for Franklin. There was not much hope of finding the explorer alive, but the mystery demanded a solution. The new commander, 53-year-old Captain Edward Belcher, was a curious choice. He had sailed with Beechey in 1825 and had done outstanding surveys in various parts of the world, but he lacked the qualities of a good commander. He was choleric, jealous of his junior officers, panicky and dull. "You may be a skillful navigator and a clever seaman," a superior once said to him after a petulant display on Belcher's part, "but a great officer you can never be with that narrow mind." Apparently, though, the Admiralty considered Belcher an adequate leader for what was essentially a lost cause.

Belcher's five-ship fleet arrived at Beechey Island in Barrow Strait on August 10. The 500-ton frigate *North Star* was to remain there as a depot ship and an emergency retreat for the crew of any vessel that got into difficulties. The remainder of the fleet split up into two groups. Belcher's flagship, the *Assistance,* and its steam tender, the *Pioneer,* headed up Wellington Channel, where they spent the winter conducting a fruitless search for further traces of the Franklin expedition. The *Resolute,* commanded by Henry Kellett, who had just returned from his stint in Bering Strait, and the tender *Intrepid,* now commanded by Leopold McClintock, steered toward Melville Island. Their instructions were to leave a cache of supplies at Winter Harbor, Parry's old anchorage, for the *Investigator,* McClure's ship. Nothing had been heard of McClure since he had entered the polar waters from the west two years before, but it was known that it was his intention to head for Winter Harbor if he got into trouble.

The *Resolute* and the *Intrepid* made their winter quarters at Dealy Island, just south of Melville Island, and McClintock promptly sent out sledge parties to establish advance food caches for the following spring's overland journeys. In mid-September, Lieutenant George Frederick Mecham of the *Resolute,* on his way back from laying one of these depots at Liddon Gulf, stopped to examine Parry's Monument and found something quite unexpected. Inside the cylinder containing the routine record that McClintock had left there the previous year was a second message, dated April 28, 1852, and signed by Robert McClure. It was a journal and a chart of the *Investigator's* voyage, and said that the ship was less than 200 miles away to the west, icebound in a bay on the north coast of Banks Island. McClure's despair was apparent: "If we should not again be heard of," he had written, "in all probability we shall have been carried into the Polar pack, or to the westward of Melville Island; in either case, any attempt to send succor would be to increase the evil, as

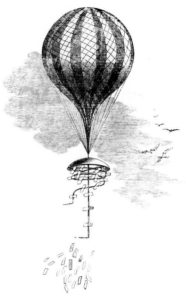

In hopes of alerting any survivors of the Franklin expedition to their presence, rescue vessels loosed hydrogen-filled balloons carrying bundles of messages stitched to lengths of fast- and slow-burning fuses. As the bundles were freed, they released showers of filled-in forms like those below, printed on bright paper.

Despatched   by a Balloon from
       H. M. S.
in Lat.   N., Long.   W.,
        To Sir John Franklin.

Despatched   by a Balloon from
       H. M. S.   Resolute
in Lat.   N., Long.   W.,
        To Sir John Franklin.

Gift buttons like this one, stamped with the locations of rescue ships and food caches, were designed to enlist Eskimos in the search for Franklin. The theory was that button-wearing Eskimos might come upon survivors, who would read the life-saving information. Unfortunately, no Eskimos turned up to set the rescue scheme in motion.

any ship that enters the Polar pack would be inevitably crushed."

Mecham hurried back with the news, but it was far too late in the season to make the westward trip. McClure must endure the winter in ignorance of the help that lay at hand. This notion caused Henry Kellett no little anxiety. McClure's note mentioned the possibility that his ship might be released in the summer that had just passed, in which case he might already be gone. But if the vessel were still imprisoned, McClure might choose to abandon it at the earliest opportunity the following spring and begin an overland trek. Were he to do so, his chances of survival were minimal. Familiar with McClure's headstrong tendencies from their encounter at Cape Lisburne two years before, Kellett realized that he had to get word to him somehow before it was too late. So on March 10, 1853—weeks earlier than any previous journey of its kind—Kellett dispatched Lieutenant Bedford Pim and two sledges toward the spot indicated by McClure's desperate message.

McClure and his men had spent their first winter locked in the ice in Prince of Wales Strait. Before the darkness set in, he had made a sledge trip up to Point Russell, on the northeast corner of Banks Island. In front of him lay the icy expanse of Melville Sound, reached by Parry from the east in 1819. He had only to sail into the sound and follow Parry's route back out into Baffin Bay to complete the Northwest Passage. This glimpse of triumph would have to sustain McClure through the long ordeal that lay ahead.

That first winter was notable for the mounting tensions among the company and for two unfortunate omissions. McClure had made little provision for recreation, and morale declined. And when the time for spring sledge journeys arrived, he neglected to send one to leave a message at Parry's Monument on Melville Island. Had he done so, it would have been found by McClintock in the late spring of 1851, and McClure would have been spared a year of torment. Still, parties dispatched along the coast of Victoria Island made useful surveys.

A team commanded by McClure himself encountered some Eskimos and inquired after Franklin. No information was forthcoming, although the missionary Miertsching carried away some lively impressions. Eskimos, he learned, believed that "while they rest at night the sun looks down on the earth through little openings"—the stars. As the sailors were leaving, McClure himself, on an unusually generous impulse, took a red shawl from his neck and wound it around that of a young woman carrying a baby. The gift perplexed her, and the reason was soon obvious. Eskimo custom required her to give something in return, and she had nothing but her baby to offer. This she did, with tears in her eyes. When McClure politely refused the gift, reported Miertsching, "she looked at the captain in a very friendly manner and laughed, delighted that she could keep her child."

July released the *Investigator* from the ice, but the northern part of the strait remained blocked. McClure now decided to double back and follow the coast of Banks Island around to the west and north, hoping to enter Melville Sound that way. Several miles of open water lay between the polar pack and the shore until they reached Cape Prince Alfred, at the northwest corner of the island. There, the pack was so close to land that the *Investigator* had to be towed around the point. A few miles farther on, the explorers were blocked. "This," wrote Miertsching, "seemed to be the end of water and the beginning of eternal ice." They were unable to move for nine days, and the bleak coast to their starboard offered little but an occasional hare and ptarmigan. Finally, the conjuction of a south-westerly gale and a high tide set them free. Against overpowering odds they tacked and hauled and blasted their way through the pack, surviving blizzard and merciless battering by the ice.

The experience sapped both their energies and their spirits. In late September the ship was making her way along the northern coast of Banks Island in an uncanny silence when the ice master climbed down from his crow's-nest and announced that he could bear the tension no more: For although they were proceeding with ghostly smoothness, wrote Miertsching, "all was ice ahead and not a spoonful of water to be seen." Even McClure lost his taciturn fortitude and the clarity of his judgment and became ever more cautious about venturing from the night's anchorage into the pack ice.

On September 24, 1851, the ship arrived at the entrance of a deep inlet that McClure later named Mercy Bay. His men were exhausted from a 30-hour battle with a gale, and he elected to put into the bay to rest. Some of the crew later claimed that, just then, there was a clearance in the central pack of Melville Sound, and that they could have got across it to Winter Harbor on Melville Island. Whatever the truth of the matter, McClure's decision was an unfortunate one. Mercy Bay iced up within days of their entry, and it would imprison the ship for two winters.

During this time, scurvy, hunger and despair were the explorers' constant lot. Two men went mad and often had to be kept in irons. Others, victims of frostbite, had their toes and fingers amputated by the surgeon. Worst of all was the hunger. Some of the explorers' meat had spoiled and, though a caribou was bagged from time to time, the uncertain future necessitated tight rations. During 1852 the weight of the men would drop by an average of 35 pounds.

In April of 1852, McClure took a sledge team across Melville Sound to Melville Island, hoping to find some sign of the Austin expedition, or at least a cache of supplies at Winter Harbor. Instead, all the cache yielded was McClintock's record that the expedition had been stuck for the winter of 1850-1851 at Griffith Island, and that no trace of Franklin had been detected near Melville Island. Realizing that Austin, with no reason to come back to Winter Harbor, was probably long gone, McClure wept. Still, he deposited his own record in Parry's Monument—for posterity if nothing else.

Summer brought no break in the ice, and McClure put the crew on even more stringent rations. As the explorers commenced their third winter in the Arctic, scurvy sent many of them into sick bay, and everyone else was "feeble, depressed, with a dull haggard stare," Miertsching recorded. With the approach of spring, McClure formed a desperate plan. Because the coming summer was no more likely to set the *Investigator* free than the previous one, he gave orders that most of the crew should leave the ship in sledges and try to make their escape to the east and the south. He and 20 of the strongest members of the crew would

Members of an expedition led by Sir Edward Belcher use sledges—adapted from an Eskimo design—in their search for Franklin in the spring of 1853. Each sledge could carry about half a ton of provisions or a large boat. Sails—and occasionally, large kites—were raised to take advantage of favoring winds.

stay behind, hoping—if a thaw did come—to extricate the ship and sail it eastward into Baffin Bay.

Virtually no one thought the captain's plan made sense. Miertsching, who had been assigned to leave with the sledges, believed that it condemned the invalid majority to almost certain death. "Twenty-one men are now in hospital," he wrote, yet "in six weeks we must, with those judged unfit to remain longer with the ship, harness ourselves to sledges laden with supplies, and drag them through snow and ice for hundreds of miles. How many of us will in this way see Europe? The answer is: No one." But McClure was adamant. The date fixed for the departure of the sledges was April 15.

On April 6, one man died—the first, in spite of all their privations, since the ship had set out more than three years before. McClure and Miertsching walked on the ice close to the ship while the man's grave was being dug, and the captain told the missionary that, though he did not expect to survive, he had no fear of death. As he was speaking, a sailor interrupted to say that a man or animal had been sighted in the distance. Another seaman ran up to say three men and a dog sledge were approaching. McClure and Miertsching walked out to meet them. From their clothes and the color of their faces, stained dark by the smoke of their lamps, the strangers appeared to be Eskimos. But one of them, when he was near enough, stunned McClure and Miertsching by calling out: "I am Lieutenant Pim, late of the *Herald*, now of the *Resolute*. Captain Kellett is with her at Dealy Island."

For the first time, an expedition that had entered the American Arctic from the east had met with one coming from the west. Part of the journey had been made on foot, of course: No ship had got through. But McClure still clung to the idea—or to the pretense—that the *Investigator* could make it home under her own power, with her own crew. Kellett had sent a letter with Pim, suggesting that McClure abandon ship if his men were too weak for such labor. But McClure was determined not to do that on his own responsibility. On April 9 he left with Pim to argue his case with Kellett, ordering Lieutenant Samuel G. Cresswell, Miertsching and two dozen of the sickliest men to follow on the 15th.

When Cresswell's pathetic group straggled into Kellett's camp on May 2, their shocking condition—shrunken bodies, hollow eyes, stumbling step—prompted Kellett to issue an order immediately: McClure should abandon the *Investigator* unless 20 volunteers strong enough to work the ship could be found among the crew. Kellett sent his own doctor back to Mercy Bay to examine the men, and his verdict was final: Fewer than 10 men could be mustered, and virtually the whole crew was incapable of further active duty.

The ship was abandoned and the whole of the *Investigator's* crew trudged or were carried nearly 200 miles across Melville Sound to Dealy Island. The weakest of the men were then sent by sledge to the depot ship *North Star* at Beechey Island. From there a ship that had brought additional supplies from England carried them home. For the rest, though their joy at rescue was inexpressible, the ordeal still was not over. Although a gale moved Kellett's vessels some 100 miles to the east, ice trapped them once again, and their occupants settled in to spend another

A flippant antidote to boredom

Wintering aboard ship in the far north—a common enough occurrence as explorers penetrated deep into the maze of the Arctic archipelago—involved mental as well as physical trials. For sheer energy-sapping, temper-fraying monotony, few places on earth could equal the polar wasteland during the six months of the year when darkness and ice reigned supreme.

But most Arctic adventurers put up a valiant battle against boredom. Rigid rules of shipboard conduct were relaxed during the winter months, with commanders condoning and even participating in gambols seldom tolerated at other times. Lively evenings of singing, dancing and card playing were often fueled by liberal rations of ale and wine. And officers and men cheerfully mingled in raucous performances on improvised stages.

On some ships, the fight against ennui was abetted by breezy, handwritten publications like the one at right. This particular journal, whimsically named *The Queens Illuminated Magazine and North Cornwall Gazette*, was produced during the winter of 1852-1853 for the edification of men aboard two ships, the *Assistance* and the *Pioneer*, jointly searching for Sir John Franklin. The magazine's editor was none other than the youthful commander of the *Pioneer*, Sherard Osborn.

Osborn's stated aim was to "avoid personalities or disputation, to be entertaining and cheap." He filled his publication with letters, poetry, playbills and announcements, many of them accompanied by drawings and cartoons (*following pages*). And he even attempted journalism of sorts, although practically the only news to report consisted of the various diversions concocted by the icebound crews. One issue told of a concert in which "the warring of the gale without formed a deep bass to the Eolian harplike sound of the band." Another described an operetta whose distraught heroine (an appropriately costumed crewman) slays the villain in defense of her honor, then—in a conclusion perfectly tailored to the audience—"gradually recovers, dances a hornpipe and, warming under the influence of the inspiriting dance, balances a bottle on her head."

The sprightly title page for the first issue of The Queens Illuminated Magazine and North Cornwall Gazette, *dated October 28, 1852, uses imaginative art to separate its handwritten columns and provide a capital D at the start of the text.*

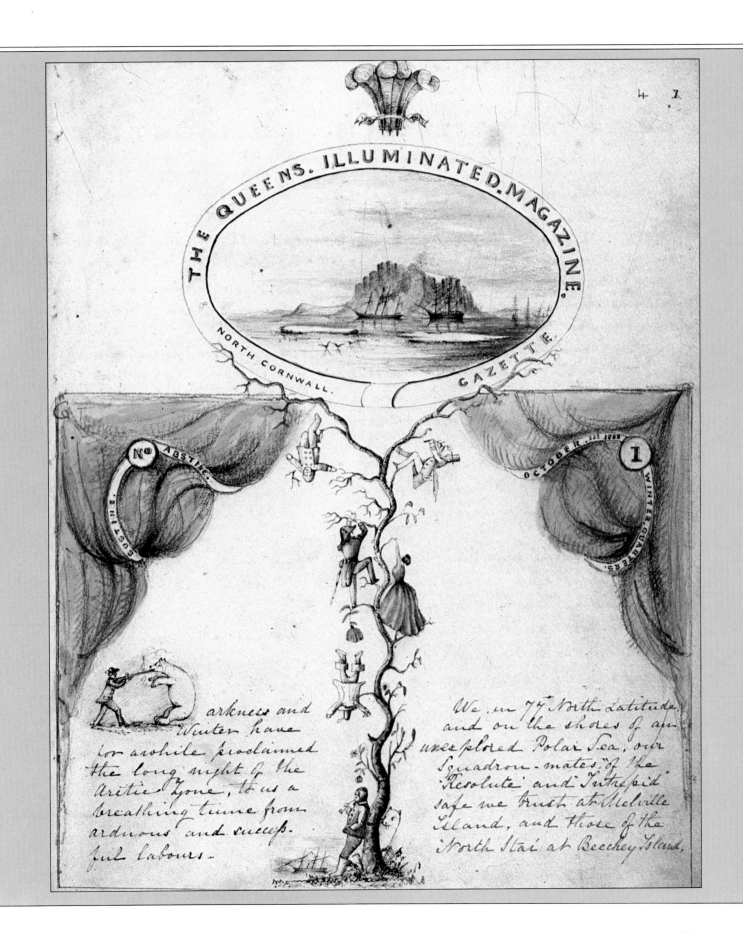

THE QUEENS. ILLUMINATED. MAGAZINE.

NORTH CORNWALL. GAZETTE.

OCTOBER 1st 1852

No 1

arkness and Winter have for awhile proclaimed the long night of the Arctic Zone, to us a breathing time from arduous and successful labours —

We in 77° North Latitude, and on the shores of an unexplored Polar Sea, our Squadron-mates of the "Resolute" and "Intrepid" safe we trust at Melville Island, and those of the North Star at Beechey Island,

In a drawing from Sherard Osborn's journal, officers while away the hours in a comfortably furnished room that is stocked with writing materials, a supply of books and a handy bottle of wine.

Seated on hard mess-room benches, four members of the crew pore over their lessons. Many of the sailors attended classes—known as "time-shorteners"— on subjects that ranged from basic mathematics to the natural sciences.

A specter representing the chill of the Arctic winter is chased away by barrels of ale. At times the temperature outside the icebound Assistance and Pioneer plummeted to as low as –60° F.

This cartoon illustrates a tongue-in-cheek definition of "editor," a word supposedly derived from a Cockney corruption of "head hitter": "One who is capable of giving hard raps and also reviews any literary work for publication."

"The conversion of broadshouldered men into sylphlike women" for their stage performances often required the combined efforts of the Assistance' bosun and his mate, a pair praised for their "subtle knowledge of that most complicated of all rigging—a Lady's."

In the rousing finale of a melodrama that was performed by the explorers, a dastardly villain receives his just deserts as the heroine swoons convincingly.

winter. Plentiful provisions and Kellett's good-natured leadership made it a pleasant one, however.

More than 200 miles farther east, the vessels under Commodore Belcher were likewise trapped, but their crews spent a less convivial winter. Belcher's bullying nature and his jealousy of his junior officers aggravated the already difficult business of maintaining morale in this dark season. By spring, one lieutenant had been relieved of duty and another put under arrest.

In early April, 1854, before the spring thaw began, Kellett sent a messenger to Beechey Island to learn exactly where Belcher's ships were. The messenger returned with a shocking order from the fleet commander: "Meet me at Beechey Island, with the crews of all vessels, before the 26th of August." Belcher had panicked and was ordering the abandonment of four of his five ships. Kellett dispatched McClintock in a sledge to make certain of the order—assuring Belcher in a private letter that he and his officers believed their ships would be freed in the summer breakup. But Belcher would not back down, and by the end of May the three crews under Kellett's command were camped near the *North Star*, where they were joined by Belcher and the crews from the *Assistance* and the *Pioneer*. Only the lucky arrival of two supply ships prevented what would have been a massively overcrowded transatlantic crossing in the *North Star*.

A subsequent court-martial—mandatory when a captain abandoned his ship, let alone a small fleet—acquitted Belcher, as gentlemanly courts-martial very often did; but the verdict was delivered in tones of icy contempt. A postscript to the episode was probably even more galling to Belcher. During the thaw of 1855, the deserted *Resolute*, freed from the ice, floated eastward and arrived, empty but unscathed, in Baffin Bay. There, an American whaler took her in tow. As a gesture of friendship, the American government refitted the ship and sent her back to England, where she was employed in a variety of commissions for some 30 more years.

A quite different reception was accorded McClure and his companions. They returned to a country embroiled in the Crimean War, and the incompetent conduct of the high command during that struggle made it desirable to create heroes. McClure was picked for such treatment, despite the fact that his travail had been caused largely by his own bad judgment. Moreover, he had been guilty of something approaching insubordination in moving into the Arctic before Collinson had caught up with him. And McClure had failed in his primary mission by adding nothing to the knowledge of Franklin's fate. (Neither had Collinson, but he brought his crew back home in the best of health and spirits.) McClure was nonetheless the man of the hour: He had, albeit in more than one ship and with a long walk between sailings, led his crew from Bering Strait to Baffin Bay. The Admiralty praised his achievement. The Queen knighted him. And Parliament, after much controversy, decided that he had achieved the goal sought by scores of explorers from Cabot onward. It awarded him £10,000 for passing through the seas of the Canadian Arctic.

But Parliament did not in fact refer to *the* Northwest Passage in its award to McClure. Rather, the award was for completion of a Northwest Passage, for during McClure's long absence another claim had come to light from a quite different source. The mystery of the Franklin expedition had been solved.

Amid the welter of naval expeditions that were sent out during the years from 1850 to 1855, one man contented himself with walking. John Rae, a native of Scotland's Orkney Islands and now surgeon to the Hudson's Bay Company, traveled incredible distances on foot. In 1851, in a journey that took him more than 5,000 miles, he traversed 700 miles of undiscovered coastline along the south of Victoria Island. While he was returning overland to the United States at the end of this epic hike, Rae covered an average of 45 miles a day. He is said to have walked a total of more than 23,000 miles in the Arctic alone during the course of his life—making maps, taking notes and collecting plants and animals even as he went his swift way.

In 1853, while still in the employment of the Hudson's Bay Company, Rae directed his extraordinary energies to the charting of the Boothia Peninsula. His interest was strictly scientific, but on this journey he made discoveries that were to eclipse those of the large and costly naval expeditions active at the same time.

Rae wintered at Repulse Bay, and then set off to the northwest with a small band of Eskimo companions. His main geographical aim was to continue the mapping of the coast between Boothia and the outlet of the little Castor and Pollux River—the point near the Back River estuary where Thomas Simpson had turned around in 1839. On April 20, 1854, in the vicinity of Pelly Bay (one of the two southern bulges of the Gulf of Boothia), an Eskimo told him that, several years before, a great number of white men had died close to the mouth of a large river, somewhere far to the west. Rae had stumbled unwittingly on the solution to the nine-year riddle. From his informant he acquired a naval officer's gilt cap band. He told the man that he would be willing to barter for similar souvenirs if they were brought to him at Repulse Bay. Then, instead of heading west to try to find the site of these deaths (he was not sure he believed the story, and in any case he had got the impression that the river was a long journey away), Rae kept to his brief and charted the coast north of the Castor and Pollux, thereby discovering something of equal importance.

What he found, and gave his name to, was the strait that—contrary to the belief of three of his predecessors in this region—separated King William Island from the west coast of Boothia. Sheltered from the winds and floes driving from the northwest, Rae Strait is the channel of water that might have brought Franklin through to success had his charts not denied its existence.

On his return trek to Repulse Bay, Rae collected more information and relics from the Eskimos, including Franklin's Order of Merit and a silver plate engraved with his name. He learned that the Eskimos had seen the white men dragging their heavy sledges down King William Island, and later had discovered their bodies on the mainland coast, along with evidence that the last survivors had resorted to cannibalism before dying in their turn.

In an encounter at Pelly Bay in 1854,
explorer John Rae receives from an Eskimo
a silver spoon bearing the crest and
initials of Francis Crozier, Franklin's
second-in-command. The Eskimos
had obtained this and other relics after
Franklin's men had starved to death
140 miles west of the bay six years earlier.

Rae now decided not to stay in the Arctic another season to find the scene of this tragedy himself, but rather to get word as quickly as possible to London. He returned to a trading post on the western shore of Hudson Bay and sent an account of his findings to the Admiralty. At least the world would know that enterprise in the Arctic had been following the wrong tracks for four years, and that any future searches should be directed toward King William Island. Informed of the colossal waste of most of its efforts and money, and aware that McClure's recent expedition had only narrowly escaped a fate similar to Franklin's, the Admiralty closed its account on the matter. There was no John Barrow or Arthur Dobbs within the circles of power to urge a final resolution of all the outstanding questions. The governing body of the world's greatest navy was sick to death of the Arctic.

Lady Franklin was not. Seeing that the government would no longer help, she decided to finance yet another expedition from her own resources. She put down £20,000 toward the purchase and fitting out of the *Fox*, a small yacht of 177 tons, with auxiliary steam power. A public subscription raised additional funds, and Leopold McClintock—now a Royal Navy captain and at 38 the highly regarded veteran of three Arctic voyages—was given command. Like the expedition's other officers, and by way of tribute to his patron and the cause she clung to, he refused to accept payment for his services.

Lady Franklin wanted three things: the rescue of any survivors; any papers that might remain despite the long years since her husband's departure and presumed death; and proof that at least some of his crewmen had reached the coast near the entrance to the Back River, as Rae's information implied—proof, in other words, that Franklin had first found the sea-lane connecting the eastern and western approaches of the Northwest Passage. Privately, McClintock entertained another hope, that the little *Fox* would be the first vessel to sail through the passage and pioneer a sea route between the Atlantic and the Pacific.

The *Fox* departed on July 1, 1857, and it was soon apparent that the luck so essential to any Arctic success was missing. In Baffin Bay, southerly winds prevented the breakup and dispersal of the ice, and the *Fox*, caught in the pack, was trapped for the winter. By the following April she had drifted helplessly more than a thousand miles to the south. The chief stoker had been killed in an accident, and the long, dark months had been passed in the knowledge that if the *Fox* had delayed her departure from England for a year she would have been in no worse position. But McClintock was remarkable not only for the skill and efficiency of his exploration; he was also a beloved leader, and he kept the crew alert and content with games, lessons and a constant example of cheerfulness. "I verily believe," he wrote in his journal after the celebration of an icebound Christmas, "I was the happiest individual on board, that happy evening." It was a fit and buoyant company that at last managed to get through Lancaster Sound in the middle of August, 1858, after gales had broken up the pack ice.

They passed Prince Regent Inlet and Somerset Island on the port side, and turned down into Peel Sound. McClintock, having grasped the significance of the relics acquired by Rae farther south, realized that a mild

Near the end of his life, a still-robust John Rae displays his collection of relics from the Franklin expedition including silverware, watchcases and coins. Most of the memorabilia he acquired from the Eskimos was turned over to the Admiralty and exhibited to a rapt public.

summer had allowed Franklin to negotiate the whole of the sound, and that the possibility of repeating this achievement depended on another such season. "All of us," he wrote as they tacked down the ice-girt channel, "in a wild state of excitement—a mingling of anxious hopes and fears." But on August 17 his hopes sank when, a mere 25 miles south of Cape Walker, the *Fox* met an impassable barrier of ice.

Trying another tack, McClintock doubled back around Somerset Island to Prince Regent Inlet. He hoped to reach the southern stretch of Peel Sound through narrow Bellot Strait, which divides Somerset from Boothia. But pack ice four miles wide at the strait's western end blocked his path. It was now clear that the main aims of the expedition would only be achieved on sledges. McClintock's cherished ambition of pioneering the passage was not to be fulfilled. Reluctantly, he settled for the winter at the eastern entrance to Bellot Strait and made plans for carrying out Lady Franklin's orders the following spring.

In mid-February, McClintock made a preliminary sledge journey to visit the Eskimo settlement first encountered by James Clark Ross when he located the North Magnetic Pole in 1831. Some of the Eskimos had souvenirs from Franklin's lost ships—silverware, buttons, a medal belonging to the *Terror's* assistant surgeon. Others reported having seen graves or bones, or having heard about an abandoned ship crushed by ice to the west of King William Island.

On April 2, 1859, three separate parties, each with two sledges, set off from the *Fox*. One charted the eastern coastline of Prince of Wales Island. Of the other two, McClintock himself went down the east side of King William Island, sending Lieutenant William Hobson, his second-in-command, to follow its western shore—a piece of generosity rarely matched in the history of Arctic exploration. McClintock knew that this was the likeliest place to find documents cached by Franklin, a coup that would almost automatically bring Hobson a promotion.

From a band of Eskimos on King William Island McClintock reaped another harvest of buttons, silver plate, embroidered cloth and weapons, and he gathered random memories of the events of 11 years before. Though no one admitted to having seen any of the crewmen alive, one old woman related a vivid tale of men who "fell down and died as they walked along." Perhaps the Eskimos were reluctant to tell all they knew from a sense of shame that they had not helped the doomed stragglers. But in that bleak environment, the small Eskimo community could not possibly have fed large numbers of extra people.

Crossing Simpson Strait, McClintock investigated the coast to the east and the west of Point Ogle, at the western side of the Back River estuary. The relics he found—a few fragments of metal and some preserved meat—were of no value in themselves, but they were sufficient to indicate that this was the place where the tenuous hopes of the last of Franklin's men had finally faded.

McClintock crossed back to King William Island on May 24 and followed its shore westward. That day, while walking along a gravel ridge above the beach, he came on a skull protruding from the snow. "It so strongly resembled a bleached rounded stone," he wrote, "that the man I called from the sledge, mistaking it for one, rested his shovel upon it, but started back with horror when the hollow sound revealed to him its true nature." Digging freed the whole skeleton, which was lying face downward, "the limbs and smaller bones either dissevered or gnawed away by small animals." From fragments of clothing—"the blue jacket with slashed sleeves and braided edging, and the pilot-cloth greatcoat with plain covered buttons"—McClintock guessed that these were the remains of a steward or an officer's servant. A notebook that was discovered among the clothes was frozen too hard to yield any further information, but it later identified the man as Harry Peglar, the captain of the foretop on the *Terror*.

At Cape Herschel, McClintock examined a cairn that had been erected by Simpson in 1839 to mark his farthest point of exploration. The cairn had been broken into and was partly demolished, undoubtedly the work of Eskimos. Nonetheless, the men looked under every stone and dug into the surrounding snow, convinced that Franklin would have deposited some document in this spot. They found nothing. "It was with a feeling of deep regret and much disappointment," McClintock later wrote, "that I left this spot without finding some certain record of those martyrs to their country's fame."

Hobson had that honor. Twelve miles west of Cape Herschel, McClintock came upon another cairn, a brand-new one, marking the point at which Hobson had turned back from his exploration of the west side of the island. The note inside, dated six days earlier, stated that Hobson had seen no signs of the wrecked ships, but that he had found, in a ruined cairn some 50 miles north, near Point Victory (named by James Clark Ross in 1830), a chilling piece of written testimony to the fate of the Franklin venture. All of the *Fox* expedition's other accomplishments—the charting of some 800 miles of coastline, the recovery of numerous relics of the lost explorers—paled beside this one sheet of paper. It contained two brief messages, written on a standard printed form requesting, in six languages, that the finder return the form to the British Admiralty or to the nearest British consul.

The first message, signed by Lieutenant Graham Gore of the *Erebus* and dated May 28, 1847, outlined the achievement of the first two years of Franklin's expedition:

"H.M. ships *Erebus* and *Terror* wintered in the ice in Lat. 70°5'N Long. 98°23'W. [This refers to the second winter, spent in the pack ice 15 miles from the coast of King William Island.] Having wintered in 1846-7 [Gore muddled his dates here; he meant 1845-1846] at Beechey Island, in Lat. 74°43'28"N., Long. 91°37'15"W., after having ascended Wellington Channel to Lat. 77° and returned by the West Side of Cornwallis Island. Sir John Franklin commanding the expedition. *All well.* Party consisting of 2 officers and 6 men left the ships on Monday 24th May, 1847."

If anything, the tone was sprightly. The progress it reported was more than any other explorers had achieved, and it obviously anticipated a release from the ice in the summer of 1847. The second message, crammed into the margins of the form, and dated almost a year later— April 25, 1848—revealed a drastic change of fortune:

"H.M. ships *Terror* and *Erebus* were deserted on the 22nd April, 5 leagues NNW of this, having been beset since 12th of September, 1846.

The officers and Crews, consisting of 105 souls, under the command of Captain F.R.M. Crozier, landed here in Lat. 69°37′42″, Long. 98°41′.'' After explaining the location of the pillar where this note would be left, it concluded: ''Sir John Franklin died on the 11th June, 1847, and the total loss by deaths in the expedition has been to this date, 9 officers and 15 men. James Fitzjames, Captain, H.M.S. *Erebus*.'' To this was appended a brief line from Crozier himself: ''and start on tomorrow 26th for Back's Fish River.''

The messages thus told, in a few simple lines, the whole story of the Franklin expedition, except for the last stage of the ordeal. Rae, with the evidence obtained from his Eskimo contacts, and McClintock, with his fragmentary findings on King William Island and the mainland, had sparingly sketched in the rest.

The voyage of the *Fox* brought to an end the second phase of intense British involvement in seeking the Northwest Passage. The first, encompassing the pioneering probes of Frobisher, Davis, Hudson, Button, Baffin, James and Foxe, had come to an end because of the limitations of contemporary ships and navigational arts. The second phase, which had lasted just over 40 eventful years, had added substantially to the Victorians' knowledge of the world they inhabited. It had contributed to the study of geography, botany, climate, the movements of oceans and the ways of the Eskimos who inhabited the Arctic. It had demonstrated that the Atlantic and the Pacific were connected by sea in both the northern and southern hemispheres, although the northern link could never be used as a trade route.

Yet, for all this achievement, and for all the excitement and suspense, joy and despair it had engendered, this second phase was abandoned in an oddly untidy condition. One expedition, McClure's, had been rewarded by Parliament for making the passage, but the journey was not made in a single ship nor without essential help from other explorers. McClintock's report, upon the return of the *Fox*, revealed that another expedition, Franklin's, had discovered an alternate link in the east-west chain and had thereby established, five years before McClure, an equally valid claim to the credit for disclosing a northwest passage. And if men who die before they can reveal their discoveries to the world cannot truly be said to have advanced their country's knowledge, there remained the rival achievement of Rae: In finding the strait that bears his name, he had come closest to fulfilling the original dream of the Northwest Passage. His seaway, at least in a good year, might allow a ship to cross from ocean to ocean without hindrance.

The return of the *Fox* in September, 1859, was followed by years of controversy over these matters. When a national monument to Sir John Franklin was raised at Waterloo Place in London, it hailed him and his company for ''completing the discovery of the North-West Passage.'' However, even such imperishable memorials could not resolve the doubts and questions that were left when Britain almost petulantly withdrew her interest from the American Arctic. The final honors were left to men of other nations.

Above all, it was Americans who continued the search for vestiges of the Franklin expedition. Charles Francis Hall, a Cincinnati journalist

During the hunt for Franklin, the dismantling of a cairn on the western shore of King William Island in 1859 revealed a tin cylinder that contained the fateful message opposite. Here the marooned explorers had paused in 1848 to lighten themselves during their desperate trek south. The area was strewn with discarded equipment, including a stack of clothing four feet high.

H. M. S. *ships Erebus and Terror*
{Wintered in the Ice in

28 of May 1847 } Lat. 70° 5' N. Long. 98° 23' W

Having wintered in 1846—7 at Beechey Island in Lat 74° 43' 28" N. Long 91° 39' 15" W After having ascended Wellington Channel to Lat 77° — and returned by the West side of Cornwallis Island.

Sir John Franklin commanding the Expedition. All well

Commander.

WHOEVER finds this paper is requested to forward it to the Secretary of the Admiralty, London, *with a note of the time and place at which it was found:* or, if more convenient, to deliver it for that purpose to the British Consul at the nearest Port.

QUICONQUE trouvera ce papier est prié d'y marquer le tems et lieu ou il l'aura trouvé, et de le faire parvenir au plutot au Secretaire de l'Amirauté Britannique à Londres.

CUALQUIERA que hallare este Papel, se le suplica de enviarlo al Secretario del Almirantazgo, en Londrés, con una nota del tiempo y del lugar en donde se halló.

EEN ieder die dit Papier mogt vinden, wordt hiermede verzogt, om het zelve, ten spoedigste, te willen zenden aan den Heer Minister van de Marine der Nederlanden in 's Gravenhage, of wel aan den Secretaris der Britsche Admiraliteit, te London, en daar by te voegen eene Nota, inhoudende de tyd en de plaats alwaar dit Papier is gevonden geworden.

FINDEREN af dette Papiir ombedes, naar Leilighed gives, at sende samme til Admiralitets Secretairen i London, eller nœrmeste Embedsmand i Danmark, Norge, eller Sverrig. Tiden og Stœdit hvor dette er fundet önskes venskabeligt paategnet.

WER diesen Zettel findet, wird hier-durch ersucht denselben an den Secretair des Admiralitets in London einzusenden, mit gefälliger angabe an welchen ort und zu welcher zeit er gefunden worden ist.

Two messages, penned a year apart on a multilingual form, solved the mystery of the Franklin expedition. Scrawled around the borders of a routine report from 1847 are the grim tidings of 1848, with an ominous postscript at upper right.

bewitched by what had now become the Franklin legend, spent most of the years from 1860 to 1869 in the Arctic, living among Eskimos, learning their language, and discovering on King William Island several isolated remains of the vanished company, including a skeleton whose gold-filled tooth enabled it to be tentatively identified as that of Lieutenant Henry Le Vesconte of the *Erebus*. Between 1878 and 1880, in the course of a sledge trip that took him more than 3,000 miles, Lieutenant Frederick Schwatka of the United States Army came upon more relics and from Eskimos learned of a small bay—Starvation Cove, not far from Point Ogle and narrowly missed by McClintock in 1859—that held the most moving testimony to the fate of the last survivors. Here, Schwatka found the bleached bones that marked the resting place of Franklin's strongest men. They had reached the mainland but could not summon the strength to walk more than a few steps inland.

The next quarter century saw activity elsewhere in the Arctic—attempts to reach the North Pole, and a successful completion of the Northeast Passage by the Swedish explorer Baron Nils Adolf Erick Nordenskjöld in a bark-rigged whaler named the *Vega*—but interest in the Northwest Passage dwindled to nothing. Thus, the world was taken by surprise when it learned in December 1905 that an obscure young Norwegian named Roald Amundsen had finally conquered the Northwest Passage, sailing through in the 47-ton steam yacht *Gjöa*.

The story of Franklin, in all its heroism, sacrifice and mystery, had first inspired the boy Amundsen to dream of such a feat. "A strange ambition burned within me to endure those same sufferings," Amundsen would later write. "I, too, would suffer in a cause." As a young man, he began a secret program of physical exercise—and slept with his windows open in the middle of the Norwegian winter—to harden himself for "the coming great adventure."

In 1894, at the age of 21, he gave up his medical studies to go to sea, and three years later he joined a Belgian expedition to the Antarctic. On his return he began preparations for his own voyage. He bought the *Gjöa*—built originally as a herring boat—and acquired, mostly on credit, provisions for five years for himself and six companions. One of his suppliers, however, demanded payment after delivering some goods. When Amundsen could not come up with the money, the tradesman threatened to have the would-be Arctic explorer arrested for debt. Late that very night—June 16, 1903—the *Gjöa* slipped out of Oslo's harbor with her full company, her ample if illicit stocks, a multitude of scientific instruments and six Eskimo dogs.

Some 10 weeks later, the *Gjöa* was steaming down Peel Sound. Dense, drenching fog had been their frequent companion since Baffin Bay, and the unreliability of their compass was a further hindrance to navigation. Amundsen had studied the records of his English predecessors, however, and knew beyond doubt the best route to follow. Conditions were as favorable as they had ever been. Peel Sound allowed them through, and by the time the sea froze in October they had found a good winter harbor in Rae Strait. There, at Gjöa Haven, as Amundsen and his party named the site, they were visited and befriended by Eskimos, descendants of

Erected in London in 1866, a bronze figure of Sir John Franklin surmounts a pedestal depicting his Arctic funeral and affirming his completion of "the discovery of the North-West Passage A.D. 1847-48."

FRANKLIN

those interviewed by James Clark Ross more than 70 years before.

Amundsen, whose whole life was to be devoted to the shattering of polar records—who would be first to reach the South Pole, who would later repeat Nordenskjöld's journey through the Northeast Passage, and who, in his last years, would succeed in flying over the North Pole—was a diligent student of those for whom Arctic conditions are the only conditions. He took careful note of the ways in which his new Eskimo friends extracted a living from their hostile surrounds: He watched them build their igloos—much more effective against cold than the huts of the foreigners—and noted their clothes, their training of dogs, and their diet, with its large proportion of fat, blubber and animal entrails, all good sources of vitamin C.

Meanwhile, he did not ignore the other scientific aspects of his expedition. If only to secure a grant from the German Marine Observatory at Hamburg, Amundsen had taken care to incorporate a serious scientific program into his plans: He proposed to fix the present location of the North Magnetic Pole, which had not been accurately done since James Clark Ross's observations in 1831. Bearings taken as they approached King William Island indicated that the Pole had not moved very far from its old location, and Gjöa Haven, only 100 miles southwest of that spot, was ideal for making magnetic observations. The wealth of data Amundsen collected there would prove exceedingly satisfying to scientists. The crew also explored the area by sledge, though they could do little more than confirm McClintock's scrupulous findings.

Amundsen was granted more time for these activities than he had anticipated or wanted: The summer of 1904 was less benign than the one before, and the Gjöa remained ice-locked for another winter. But the following summer their luck returned. At 3 a.m. on August 13, 1905, the little ship slipped out of her winter haven to continue her westward course. The next two weeks were harrowing. "We jumped, so to speak, right into the same doubtful navigation as before," Amundsen remembered, "impenetrable fog, no compass and a very changeable breeze, which was therefore a poor guide." The water was so shallow and the bottom so unpredictable that soundings were made continuously. At one point, he recorded, "we were in the midst of a most disconcerting chaos; sharp stones faced us on every side, low-lying rocks of all shapes, and we bungled through zigzag, as if we were drunk." The helmsman had to keep his eye constantly on the lookout as he "jumped about in the crow's-nest like a maniac, throwing his arms about for starboard and port respectively."

For the next two weeks Amundsen was keyed to such a pitch of anxiety that he rarely ate or slept. "Here in these troublesome waters we were running the risk of spoiling the whole of our so far successful enterprise," he wrote. "All our precautions and everybody's careful attention notwithstanding, any moment might have some surprise in store for us. I could not eat. At every mealtime I felt a devouring hunger, but I was unable to swallow my food." The voyage took such a toll on the 33-year-old Amundsen that those who met him shortly afterward reported that he looked like a man in his sixties.

At last, on August 27, 1905, as the Gjöa was passing between Cape

Parry on the Canadian mainland and Nelson Head on Banks Island, the sign they had so long awaited finally appeared. Shortly after 8 a.m., as Amundsen was getting to sleep after his watch, First Lieutenant Godfred Hansen burst into the cabin. "Vessel in sight, sir!" he shouted, and ran back on deck, leaving the captain of the *Gjöa* to savor his triumph alone. "The Northwest Passage had been accomplished," Amundsen later wrote, "my dream from childhood. This very moment it was fulfilled." The ship was the *Charles Hanson*, an American whaler sailing out of San Francisco and heading toward Banks Island to search for whales. "Where its deep belly had floated, we could float," Amundsen wrote. "Victory was ours!"

There was to be one last frustration, however. The *Gjöa* had barely passed the mouth of the Mackenzie when the onset of winter trapped her once again—and trapped the whaler as well. Amundsen was so impatient for the world to learn of his achievement that on October 24 he left the ship and struck off overland into the interior of Alaska, crossing the 9,000-foot Brooks Range, then following the Porcupine and Yukon Rivers. Six weeks and 500 miles later, he arrived at an American Army post at Eagle, about 200 miles east of Fairbanks, where he sent out the news by telegraph. By the time he had returned to the *Gjöa* and had completed

The Gjöa sails into Nome, Alaska, in 1906, having completed her conquest of the Northwest Passage. Measuring 70 feet at the water line, she was about the size of the ships that first sought a waterway to the Orient 400 years earlier.

A weary Roald Amundsen, far left, joins his crew for a shipboard photograph shortly after the Gjöa's arrival in Nome. Five years later, Amundsen further proved his prowess as an explorer by becoming the first man to arrive at the South Pole.

the passage through Bering Strait to Nome, Alaska, and on to San Francisco, Amundsen was famous. The fees he commanded for lectures and appearances in the United States and Europe soon enabled him to repay his debts in Norway.

Amundsen's exploit had been brilliant. Yet without the distinctions he earned later he would probably no longer be remembered, for his was a belated postscript to an age of attainment. Behind his success lay the trials and suffering, heroism and doggedness of generations of explorers, British for the most part, whose failures had been the foundation for this ultimate triumph.

Amundsen's achievement capped a 400-year quest that, in the end, offered no intrinsic reward. Yet the Arctic continued—and continues—to cast a spell on all who glimpse it. The winds still lash, the waves still heave as furiously as they did in Frobisher's and Hudson's days, the ice still piles itself into terrifying towers. And seamen still return to it—in whalers, seal boats, weather ships, submarines. In allowing men to win the goal they had so long striven for, the Arctic yielded nothing. It remains a chimera, a compelling vision, as elusive and mysterious as when it seemed to hold in its cold grasp the key to the boundless treasure of the Orient.

A series of breakthroughs in the wake of the "Gjöa"

Roald Amundsen's successful transit of the Northwest Passage at the beginning of the 20th Century did not end exploration in the area. Mariners have continued to challenge the ice-choked waters ever since, testing out new vessels and routes, and chalking up some impressive feats of their own.

Canada entered the record book in dramatic fashion during the Second World War. In 1942, Sergeant Henry Larsen, captain of the 88-ton Mounted Police schooner *St. Roch* (left), became the first man to complete the passage from west to east, taking 28 months to travel from Vancouver to Halifax, Nova Scotia. Then, for good measure, he turned around and made the return trip in a single season.

Amundsen and Larsen owed their success partly to the maneuverability of their small vessels, partly to their navigational skills, partly to luck and good weather. To be less at the mercy of climate and ice, however, later explorers began to tackle the passage in more powerful and sophisticated ships. In 1954 the *Labrador*, a 6,500-ton Canadian icebreaker, attacked the ice head on, plowing through the passage in only 68 days. Three years later the *Labrador* teamed up with an American icebreaker and two tenders to chart a new route for deep-draft vessels; they went by way of Bellot Strait, which separates Somerset Island and Boothia Peninsula. In 1960 a U.S. submarine, the *Seadragon*, pioneered another passage; she groped her way under the polar ice with the aid of sonar and a 19th Century journal.

The most massive assault on the ice-locked north came in 1969, when a consortium of oil companies set out to determine whether oil could be shipped profitably to America's East Coast from the North Slope of Alaska. The companies spent $40 million on the venture, equipping the 150,000-ton tanker *Manhattan* with a 43,000-horsepower engine and a special ice-breaking bow. The giant tanker—17 times larger than any ship to attempt the passage previously—bullied her way to the oil fields in record time. On the return trip, however, her expensive hull was holed by ice, and plans to use the passage for profit—the hope that had lured the very first explorers—were abandoned once more.

Three members of the St. Roch expedition dig their vessel out of ice that imprisoned her for two winters during her eastward voyage. The most difficult moments came in August 1942, when the schooner was so continuously buffeted by floes that Larsen admitted he almost "gave up hope of ever getting out."

Her wood hull bearing scars from the battle with ice, the St. Roch ties up in Halifax in 1942 at the end of her eastward voyage through the passage. Wind and a 150-horsepower engine provided the propulsion for the trip. The little schooner made better time on the return journey by exchanging her original engine for one twice as powerful.

The Canadian icebreaker Labrador—the first deep-draft ship to travel through the Northwest Passage—pauses near Ellesmere Island in 1954.

During the joint U.S.-Canadian voyage by way of Bellot Strait in 1957, two ships collide amid floes. Their route cut hundreds of miles off the former deep-draft passage north of Somerset Island.

Members of the U.S.-Canadian expedition are lowered to the ice on concrete blocks. The blocks were normally swung about by a boom to rock the ship and aid in ice breaking.

Traveling through the Northwest Passage in 1960, the United States nuclear submarine Seadragon surfaces in Baffin Bay. At one point in the voyage, the submarine dived directly under an iceberg in order to determine its contours.

In a picture taken through the Seadragon's periscope, crewmen prepare to study the polar ice. Although the submarine usually surfaced only for serious purposes, she came up at the North Pole so the men could play baseball—one of the more frivolous firsts in the annals of Northwest Passage exploration.

As two escorting icebreakers stand by, the 1,000-foot-long oil tanker Manhattan plows through the ice—which promptly closes in behind her. Endowed with a

specially designed bow that allowed her to ride up on the ice and crush it, the vessel forged through the passage at speeds of five to eight knots.

Picture Credits

The sources for the illustrations in this book are shown below. Credits from left to right are separated by semicolons, from top to bottom by dashes.
Cover: Peabody Museum of Salem. Front and back endpapers: Drawing by Peter McGinn.
3: Derek Bayes, courtesy National Maritime Museum, London. 6, 7: National Museum of American Art, Smithsonian Institution, gift of Eleanor Blodgett. 8, 9: Courtesy Old Dartmouth Historical Society. 10, 11: Mark Sexton, courtesy Dr. Richard Fitton. 12, 13: Dallas Museum of Fine Arts, Anonymous Gift. 14, 15: Courtesy City Art Gallery, Bristol, England. 17: Stephen J. Kovacik, courtesy Massachusetts Historical Society. 20, 21: Photo Bulloz, courtesy Musée National des Châteaux de Versailles et de Trianon, France, insert, Photo Bulloz, courtesy Musées de Saint-Malo, France. 22: By permission of the British Library, London (No. 566.i.14). 25: Maps by Bill Hezlep. 27: By permission of the British Library, London (No. 48.h.I8). 28: Bodleian Library, Oxford, England. 30: Rare Books and Manuscripts Division, New York Public Library, Astor, Lenox and Tilden Foundations. 33: Courtesy of the Trustees of the British Museum, London. 34: By permission of the Houghton Library, Harvard University. 36: By permission of the British Library, London (No. C.54.bb.33). 38-43: Rare Books and Manuscripts Division, New York Public Library, Astor, Lenox and Tilden Foundations. 44: Historical Section, Naval Staff, The Hague, courtesy Holland Society of New York. 46, 47: The Peabody Museum of Salem. 48: By kind permission of the Benchers of the Honourable Society of the Middle Temple, London. 50: Maps by Bill Hezlep. 54: The Tate Gallery, London. 57: Stanley Travers and Partners, Wales, courtesy Sir Cennydd Traherne, KG. 59: By permission of the British Library, London (No. 679.h.I3). 60: By permission of the British Library, London (Add.MS. 12206.ff.2v-3). 64: Det Kongelige Bibliotek, Billedsamlingen, Copenhagen. 66-68: Courtesy Hudson's Bay Company, Canada. 69: By permission of the British Library, London (No. C32.e.I6). 73, 75: By permission of the British Library, London (Nos. 70095.(7), 674.g.20). 76, 77: Maps by Bill Hezlep. 78: Picture Collection, The Branch Libraries, New York Public Library, Astor, Lenox and Tilden Foundations. 79: Rare Books and Manuscripts Division, New York Public Library, Astor, Lenox and Tilden Foundations. 81: General Research Division, New York Public Library, Astor, Lenox and Tilden Foundations. 82: Picture Division, Public Archives of Canada, Ottawa (Negative No. C-18504)—Hillel Burger, Peabody Museum, Harvard University. 84, 85: Derek Bayes, courtesy National Maritime Museum, London. 86-93: Drawings by Richard Schlecht. 94-97: Library of Congress. 98, 99: Library of Congress—Derek Bayes, courtesy Scott Polar Research Institute, Cambridge, England (No. 59/3/12). 101: Derek Bayes, Hertfordshire, courtesy P. E. Parry, Furneux Pelham, Hertfordshire, England. 102, 103: Derek Bayes, courtesy Scott Polar Research Institute, Cambridge, England (Nos. 56/14, 72/6/16). 104, 105: Maps by Bill Hezlep. 107-109: Library of Congress. 110: National Portrait Gallery, London. 111-117: Library of Congress. 118-125: Derek Bayes, courtesy Scott Polar Research Institute, Cambridge, England (Nos. 66/3/48, 66/3/63, 66/3/47, 66/3/2, 66/3/76, 66/3/43, 66/3/30, 66/3/75, 66/3/68, 66/3/70, 66/3/60, 66/3/72, 66/3/62). 126, 127: Library of Congress. 128: National Portrait Gallery, London. 129: General Research Division, New York Public Library, Astor, Lenox and Tilden Foundations. 131: Maps by Bill Hezlep. 132: Scott Polar Research Institute, Cambridge, England (No. 74/43/I). 133: National Maritime Museum, London—Scott Polar Research Institute, Cambridge, England (Nos. 74/43/23, 74/43/9). 135-137: Drawings by John Batchelor. 138-140: National Portrait Gallery, London. 142, 143: Peabody Museum of Salem. 144: Derek Bayes, courtesy Scott Polar Research Institute, Cambridge, England (No. 1228). 145: Courtesy New York Public Library, Astor, Lenox and Tilden Foundations. 146: Derek Bayes, courtesy National Maritime Museum, London—Derek Bayes, courtesy Scott Polar Research Institute, Cambridge, England (No. 1057). 147: Derek Bayes, courtesy Scott Polar Research Institute, Cambridge, England (No. 1233). 149: Derek Bayes, courtesy National Maritime Museum, London. 151-153: By permission of the British Library, London (Nos. Add.MS. 35305.f.4, 35305.f.40, 35305.f.4v, 35305.f.26v, 35305.f.25v, 35305.f.20v, 35305.f.53). 156, 157: Courtesy Hudson's Bay Company, Canada. 160: Culver Pictures. 161: Derek Bayes, courtesy National Maritime Museum, London. 162: Derek Bayes, London. 164, 165: Courtesy Bancroft Library, University of California, Berkeley. 166: St. Roch Historical Site, Parks Canada. 167: Picture Division, Public Archives of Canada, Ottawa (Negative No. PA121392). 168: Picture Division, Public Archives of Canada, Ottawa (Negative No. PA108008)—National Archives (Negative Nos. 26-G-5784, 26-G-5788). 169: U.S. Navy. 170, 171: Dan Guravich.

Acknowledgments

The index for this book was prepared by Gale Linck Partoyan. The editors wish to thank the following: John Batchelor, artist, and David Lyon, consultant *(pages 34-37)*; Peter McGinn, artist *(endpaper maps)*; Richard Schlecht, artist, and William Avery Baker, consultant *(pages 86-93)*.

For their help in the preparation of this book, the editors also wish to thank: In Canada: Winnipeg, Manitoba—Alec Ross, Classification Archivist, Hudson's Bay Company Archives. In France: Dieppe—Pierre Bazin, Curator, Musée de Dieppe; Paris—Claude Bellarbre, Librarian; Jacques Chantriot; Marjolaine Mathikine, Director for Historical Studies; Marcel Redouté, Curator; Catherine Touny, Musée de la Marine; Françoise Lapadu-Harques, Curator, Bibliothèque Nationale; Monique de la Roncière; Saint-Malo—Dan Lallier, Curator, Musée de Saint-Malo. In Germany: Munich—Sarah Patee. In Northern Ireland: Carrickfergus—John McClintock. In the United Kingdom: Addington—Surrey Ronald Thomas; Cambridge—Clive Holland, Scott Polar Research Institute; Hull—Arthur G. Credland, Town Docks Museum; Dr. Michael Lewis; London—Christine Kelly, H. G. Bilcliffe, Deborah Barrett, Royal Geographical Society; Clare Austin, Department of Manuscripts; Dr. H. M. Wallis and Sara J. Tyacke, Map Room; Ray Cassidy, Photographic Service; Graham Marsh, Photographic Section, British Library; R. Williams, Department of Prints and Drawings, The British Museum; Bridget Clifford and Caroline Roberts, John Munday, Rena Prentice, Pat Blanckett, Department of Weapons and Antiquities; R.J.B. Knight, Department of Manuscripts; Joan Moore and John D. Fisher, Department of Photographic Sales; A.W.H. Pearsall, Historical Section; Stephen M. Riley, Department of Ships; Denis S. Stonham, Department of Historical Photographs; Barbara Tomlinson and Roger Quarm, Picture Department; Dr. A. Hood, Lt. Cdr. C.C.W. Tervell, Ann Shuley, Department of Navigation and Astronomy, National Maritime Museum; Ann Parry.

The editors also wish to thank: In the United States: Washington, D.C.—John Ulrich and Staff, Navigation Department, Defense Mapping Agency; New York—Lawrence Murphy and Staff, Rare Book Division, New York Public Library.

Bibliography

Allen, Oliver E., and the Editors of Time-Life Books, *The Pacific Navigators* (The Seafarers series). Time-Life Books, 1980.

Amundsen, Roald, *My Life as an Explorer.* Doubleday Page, 1927.

The Northwest Passage. Vols. 1 and 2. London: Archibald Constable, 1908.

Asher, George Michael, *Henry Hudson the Navigator: The Original Documents in Which His Career is Recorded, Collected, Partly Translated, and Annotated, with an Introduction.* London: Hakluyt Society, 1860.

Back, George, *Narrative of the Arctic Land Expedition to the Mouth of the Great Fish River, and along the Shores of the Arctic Ocean, in the Years 1833, 1834, and 1835.* Charles E. Tuttle, 1970.

Narrative of an Expedition in H.M.S. Terror Undertaken with a View to Geographical Discovery on the Arctic Shores in the Years 1836-7. London: John Murray, 1838.

Barrow, John, *A Chronological History of Voyages into the Arctic Regions.* London: John Murray, 1818.

Beaglehole, J. C., *The Life of Captain James Cook.* Stanford University Press, 1974.

Cameron, Ian, *To the Farthest Ends of the Earth.* London: Macdonald, 1980.

Carrington, C. E., *The British Overseas.* Cambridge University Press, 1968.

Chiappelli, Fredi, *First Images of America,* Vols. 1 and 2. University of California Press, 1972.

Chidsey, Donald Barr, *Sir Humphrey Gilbert: Elizabeth's Racheteer.* Harper and Brothers, 1932.

Christy, Miller, *The Voyages of Captain Luke Foxe and Captain Thomas James,* Vols. 1 and 2. London: Hakluyt Society, 1894.

Collinson, Richard, *The Three Voyages of Martin Frobisher.* London: Hakluyt Society, 1867.

Cooke, Alan and Clive Holland, *The Exploration of Northern Canada.* Arctic History Press, 1978.

Courtauld, Augustine, *From the Ends of the Earth: An Anthology of Polar Writings.* London: Oxford University Press, 1958.

Cumming, William P., Raleigh A. Skelton, and David Quinn, *The Discovery of North America.* American Heritage, 1972.

Cyriax, Richard J., *Sir John Franklin's Last Arctic Expedition: A Chapter in the History of the Royal Navy.* London: Methuen, 1939.

Delpar, Helen, *The Discoverers.* McGraw-Hill, 1980.

De Veer, Gerrit, *The Three Voyages of William Barents to the Arctic Regions.* Burt Franklin, 1853.

Dictionary of National Biography. London: Oxford University Press, 1968.

Dodge, Ernest S., *Northwest by Sea.* Oxford University Press, 1961.

The Polar Rosses: John and James Clark Ross and Their Explorations. Harper & Row, 1973.

Ferris, Mary L. D., "Henry Hudson the Navigator." *Magazine of American History,* September 1893.

Fisher, Robin and Hugh Johnston, *Captain James Cook and His Times.* Vancouver: Douglas & McIntyre, 1979.

Foss, Michael, *Tudor Portraits.* Barnes and Noble, 1974.

Franklin, John, *Narrative of a Second Expedition to the Shores of the Polar Sea, in the Years 1825, 1826, and 1827.* Carey, Lea, and Carey, 1828.

Gerson, Noel B., *Passage to the West: The Great Voyages of Henry Hudson.* Julian Messner, 1968.

Golder, F. A., *Bering's Voyages: An Account of the Efforts of the Russians to Determine the Relation of Asia and America,* Vol. 1. American Geographical Society, 1922.

Harrisse, Henry, *John Cabot the Discoverer of North America.* Argosy-Antiquarian, 1968.

Hearne, Samuel, *A Journey from Prince of Wales's Fort in Hudson Bay to the Northern Ocean in the Years 1769, 1770, 1771 and 1772.* J. B. Tyrrell, ed. Toronto: Champlain Society, 1911.

Hoffman, Bernard G., *Cabot to Cartier.* Toronto: University of Toronto Press, 1961.

"Hudson and his Exploration of the Hudson River." *Scientific American,* September 25, 1909.

Hyde, Alexander, *The Frozen Zone and Its Explorers.* Columbian Book Company, 1874.

Janvier, Thomas, "New Data concerning Henry Hudson." *Harper's Weekly,* September 25, 1909.

Jenkins, James, *A History of the Whale Fisheries,* Kennikat Press, 1971.

Kane, Elisha Kent, *Arctic Explorations: The Second Grinnell Expedition in Search of Sir John Franklin,* Vol. 2. Childs & Peterson, 1856.

Kirwan, L. P., *A History of Polar Exploration.* W. W. Norton, 1960.

Lamb, W. Kaye, ed., *The Journals and Letters of Sir Alexander Mackenzie.* Macmillan, 1970.

Leacock, Stephen, *Adventurers of the Far North, a Chronicle of the Frozen Seas.* Toronto: Glasgow, Brook, 1914.

Lloyd, Christopher, *Mr. Barrow of the Admiralty, a Life of Sir John Barrow 1764-1848.* London: Collins, 1970.

Lyon, Captain George, *A Brief Narrative of an Unsuccessful Attempt to Reach Repulse Bay through Sir Thomas Rowe's "Welcome," in His Majesty's Ship Griper.* London: John Murray, 1825.

Mackie, J. D., *The Earlier Tudors.* Oxford University Press, 1952.

Markham, Albert Hastings, *The Voyages and Works of John Davis: The Navigator.* London: Hakluyt Society, 1880.

Markham, Sir Clements R., *The Lands of*

Silence a History of Arctic and Antarctic Exploration. London: Cambridge University Press, 1921.

A Life of John Davis, the Navigator, 1550-1605, Discoverer of Davis Straits. London: George Phillip and Son, 1889.

The Voyages of William Baffin, 1612-1622. Burt Franklin, Hakluyt Society, 1881.

Martin, Chester, "The Beaver." *The Royal Charter,* June 1945.

McClure, Robert John, *The Discovery of the Northwest Passage.* Sherard Osborn, ed. Charles E. Tuttle, 1969.

McDougall, George F., *The Eventful Voyage of H. M. Discovery Ship "Resolute" to the Arctic Regions.* London: Longman, Brown, Green, Longmans, & Roberts, 1857.

Morrison, Samuel Eliot, *The European Discovery of America: The Northern Voyages.* London: Oxford University Press, 1971.

Mountfield, David, *A History of Polar Exploration.* Dial, 1974.

Mowat, Farley, *Ordeal by Ice.* Little, Brown, 1960.

Nanton, Paul, *Arctic Breakthrough: Franklin's Expeditions 1819-1847.* London: William Kimber, 1970.

Neatby, Leslie H., *Frozen Ships: The Arctic Diary of Johann Miertsching 1850-1854.* St. Martin's Press, 1967.

In Quest of the North West Passage. London: Constable, 1958.

The Search for Franklin. Walker, 1970.

Osborn, Sherard, *Stray Leaves from an Arctic Journal.* William Blackwood and Sons, 1865.

Parry, Ann, *Parry of the Arctic, the Life Story of Admiral Sir Edward Parry 1790-1855.* London: Chatto & Windus, 1963.

Parry, J. H., *The Age of Reconnaissance.* World Publishing, 1963.

Parry, William Edward, *Journal of a Second Voyage for the Discovery of a Northwest Passage.* John Murray, 1824.

Journal of a Voyage for the Discovery of a Northwest Passage from the Atlantic to the Pacific; Performed in the Years 1819-1820. Abraham Small, 1821.

Partridge, Bellamy, *Amundsen: The Splendid Norseman.* Frederick A. Stokes, 1929.

Penrose, Boies, *Travel and Discovery in the Renaissance 1420-1620.* Atheneum, 1962.

Powys, Llewelyn, *Henry Hudson.* London: John Lane the Bodley Head, 1927.

Purchas, Samuel, *Purchas His Pilgrimes,* Vols. 12 and 14. Macmillan, 1906.

Quinn, David Beers, *The Discovery of North America.* American Heritage, 1971.

The New American World, Vol. 4. Arno, 1979.

North American Discovery, circa 1000-1612. University of South Carolina Press, 1971.

The Voyages and Colonising Enterprises

of Sir Humphrey Gilbert. London: Hakluyt Society, 1940.

Rasky, Frank, The Polar Voyagers. McGraw-Hill Ryerson, 1976.

Rich, E. E., The Publications of the Hudson's Bay Record Society, Hudson's Bay Company 1670-1870, Vol. 1. 1670-1763. London: Hudson's Bay Record Society.

Ross, John, Voyage of Discovery, Exploring Baffin's Bay, and Inquiring into the Probability of a North-West Passage. London: John Murray, 1819.

Appendix to the Narrative of a Second Voyage in Search of a North-West Passage and of a Residence in the Arctic Regions, during the Years 1829, 1830, 1831, 1832, Vol. 2. London: A. W. Webster, 1835.

Narrative of a Second Voyage in Search of North-West Passage, and of a Residence in the Arctic Regions. London: A. W. Webster, 1835.

Rundall, Thomas, ed., Narratives of Voyages towards the North-West, in Search of a Passage to Cathay and India, 1496-1631. Burt Franklin, Hakluyt Society, 1849.

Shillinglaw, John J., A Narrative of Arctic Discovery, from the Earliest Period to the Present Time. London: William Shoberl, 1851.

Simpson, Thomas, Narrative of the Discoveries on the North Coast of America: Effected by the Officers of the Hudson's Bay Company during the Years 1836-39. London: Richard Bentley, 1843.

Skelton, Raleigh Ashlin, Explorers' Maps: Chapters in the Cartographic Record of Geographical Discovery. London: Routledge and Kegan Paul, 1958.

Smith, James K., Alexander Mackenzie, Explorer. Canada: McGraw-Hill Ryerson, 1973.

Smith, Whitney, The Flag Book of the United States. William Morrow, 1970.

Speck, Gordon, Samuel Hearne and the Northwest Passage. Caxton Printers, 1963.

Steele, George, Seadragon: Northwest under the Ice. Dutton, 1962.

Stefánsson, Vilhjálmur, Unsolved Mysteries of the Arctic. Books for Libraries Press, 1966.

Taylor, E.G.R., Tudor Geography 1485-1583. Octagon, 1968.

Thomson, George Malcolm, The Search for the Northwest Passage. Macmillan, 1975.

Van der Kooij, J. A., "Saga of the Half Moon of 1909: I." De Halve-Maen, The Holland Society of New York, Fall, 1977. "Saga of the Half Moon of 1909: II." De Halve-Maen, The Holland Society of New York, Winter, 1977-1978.

Wallis, Helen M., "The First English Globe: A Recent Discovery." Reprinted in The Geographical Journal, September 1951.

"Further Light on the Molyneux Globes." Reprinted in The Geographical Journal, September 1955.

Waters, David W., The Art of Navigation in England in Elizabethan and Early Stuart Times. London: Hollis and Carter, 1958.

Watson, J. Steven, The Reign of George III 1760-1815. Oxford University Press, 1960.

Williams, Glyndwr, The British Search for the Northwest Passage in the Eighteenth Century. London: Bowering, 1962.

The Expansion of Europe in the Eighteenth Century, Overseas Rivalry, Discovery and Exploitation. London: Blanford, 1966.

Williamson, James A., Maritime Enterprises 1485-1558. London: Oxford University Press, 1913.

The Voyages of the Cabots and the Discovery of North America. Da Capo, 1970.

Wilmerding, John, William Bradford: Artist of the Arctic. Catalogue for Decodova Museum and Whaling Museum of New Bedford for Exhibitions, 1969-1970.

Wright, Noel, Quest for Franklin. London: Heinemann, 1959.

Index

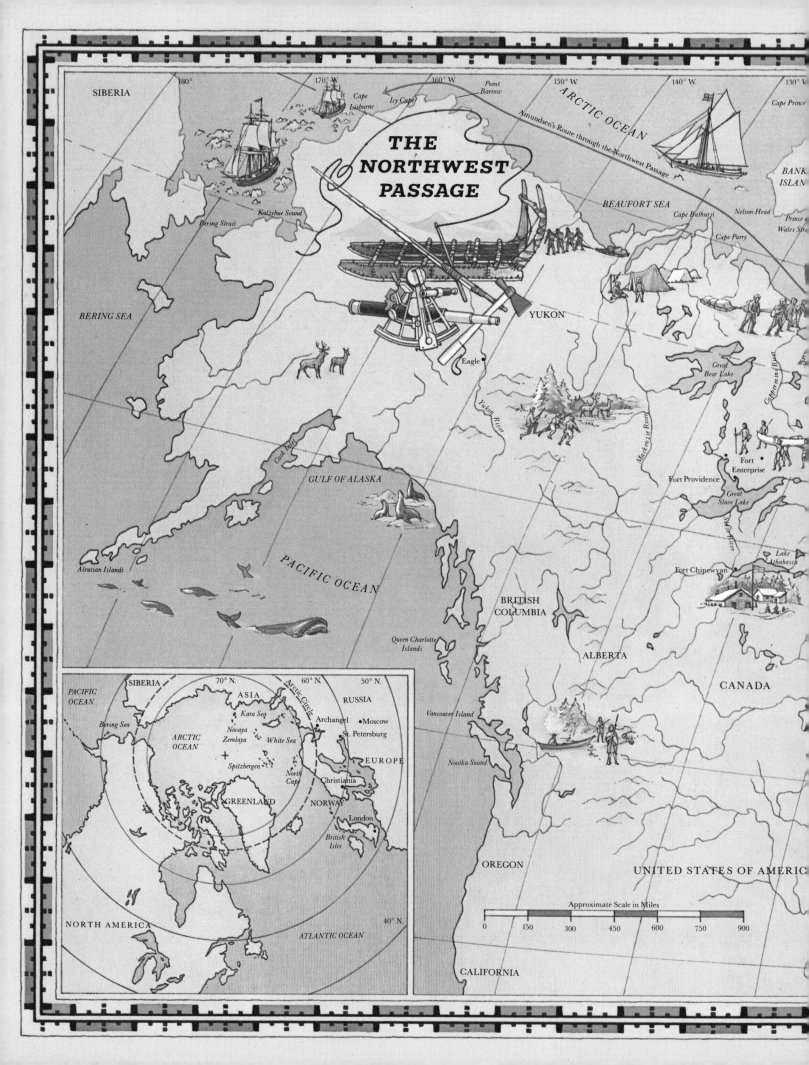

THE
NORTHWEST
PASSAGE

SIBERIA

180°

170° W.

Cape Lisburne

Icy Cape

160° W.

Point Barrow

150° W.

ARCTIC OCEAN

140° W.

130° W

Cape Prince

Amundsen's Route through the Northwest Passage

BEAUFORT SEA

Cape Bathurst

Nelson Head

BANK
ISLAND

Cape Parry

Prince
Wales Str

Kotzebue Sound

Bering Strait

BERING SEA

YUKON

Eagle

Great
Bear Lake

Coppermine River

Fort
Enterprise

Fort Providence

Great
Slave Lake

Slave River

Mackenzie River

Yukon River

Cook Inlet

GULF OF ALASKA

Fort Chipewyan

Lake
Athabasca

Aleutian Islands

PACIFIC OCEAN

BRITISH
COLUMBIA

ALBERTA

CANADA

Queen Charlotte
Islands

Vancouver Island

Nootka Sound

OREGON

UNITED STATES OF AMERICA

CALIFORNIA

Inset map

PACIFIC
OCEAN

SIBERIA

70° N.

ASIA

Kara Sea

Novaya
Zemlaya

Arctic Circle

60° N.

50° N.

RUSSIA

Archangel

Moscow

White Sea

St. Petersburg

Bering Sea

ARCTIC
OCEAN

Spitzbergen

North
Cape

EUROPE

Christiania

NORWAY

GREENLAND

London

British
Isles

NORTH AMERICA

40° N.

ATLANTIC OCEAN

Approximate Scale in Miles

0   150   300   450   600   750   900